SHORT WALK

Cornish
Pubs

Eleanor Smith

COUNTRYSIDE BOOKS
NEWBURY, BERKSHIRE

COUNTRYSIDE BOOKS
3 Catherine Road
Newbury, Berkshire

ISBN 1 85306 329 0

To my family

Cover illustration by Colin Doggett
Photographs by the author

Produced through MRM Associates Ltd., Reading
Typeset by Paragon Typesetters, Clwyd
Printed by J. W. Arrowsmith Ltd., Bristol

Contents

Area map showing locations of the walks.

Introduction

A family walk is becoming increasingly popular. More leisure time has created an interest in outdoor pursuits and what can be better than a walk based on a good pub?

The inns and taverns of Cornwall have a long history. Many have walled-up smugglers' tunnels while others started life as a 'Kiddleywink' – these were private beer houses where the landlord brewed his own potent ale. This county of legends and folklore, where fact and fiction, myth and magic blend happily together, creates a unique atmosphere for both resident and holidaymaker. Changing lifestyles have brought a challenge to Cornish publicans, many of whom have had to address themselves to a compromise between local comfort and seasonal holiday trade. Charming creekside villages have their unspoilt 'local', moorland inns have slate floored rooms and open fireplaces, while the vast surfing beaches create a need for a lively, cosmopolitan style of pub. Walkers are welcome everywhere.

In this book of 20 pub walks for the family I have chosen those establishments which can offer a family room or area where children feel comfortable and welcome. An outdoor, safe play place has been an added asset. The provision of good food at reasonable prices and well-kept ales to please the adults has also been considered. A nearby place or feature of particular interest can be found at many of the locations.

The walks all use official rights of way. They are low in mileage and on well-defined footpaths and should be suitable for most family groups. Children should, of course, be carefully controlled when using any coastal paths. Sketch maps are provided for all the routes and the relevant Ordnance Survey Landranger number is given.

Equipment: On these short walks it is not necessary to wear other than normal casual clothes, although sensible shoes or boots are a must.

Beaches: When beach walking always make yourself familiar with the state of the tide. Tide charts can be bought quite cheaply from most newsagents. NEVER walk round a jutting headland at beach level on a rising tide.

Cliff paths: These are subject to erosion. Care should be taken during and after stormy weather.

The Country Code should be observed at all times and is as follows:

Enjoy the countryside and respect its life and work.
Guard against all risk of fire.
Fasten all gates.
Keep dogs under close control.
Keep to public paths across farmland.
Use gates and stiles to cross fences, hedges and walls.
Take your litter home.
Help to keep all water clean.
Protect wildlife, plants and trees.
Take special care on country roads.
Make no unnecessary noise.

Enjoy the hospitality of the chosen pubs and walk some of the footpaths and byways of this lovely county.

Eleanor Smith
Spring 1995

Publisher's Note

We hope that you obtain considerable enjoyment from this book; great care has been taken in its preparation. However, changes of landlord and actual closures are sadly not uncommon. Likewise, although at the time of publication all routes followed public rights of way or permitted paths, diversion orders can be made and permissions withdrawn.

We cannot of course be held responsible for such diversion orders and any resultant inaccuracies in the text which result from these or any other changes to the routes nor any damage which might result from walkers trespassing on private property. We are anxious that all details covering the walks and the pubs are kept up to date and would therefore welcome information from readers which would be relevant to future editions.

Bramley
① Bude
The Carriers Inn

This 16th century building, originally three cottages, is known to have served the community as an inn for over 300 years. The attractive colourwashed pub, which overlooks the river, must have seen vast changes in the lifestyle of this area. Through an Act of Parliament, passed in 1774, it was hoped to construct a canal from Bude to Calstock, in the Tamar valley, to assist with the transporting of sand across the county. High in lime content, Bude sand was used to sweeten the acid fields of north Cornwall. Lime, too, was an important commodity for the same purpose. It was brought into Bude and unloaded onto the beach, and a canal would be of great benefit in saving time and money in transportation costs. However, the canal never reached Calstock. It did get as far as Launceston and the effect of this waterway helped to reduce the price of sand by up to three-quarters. The canal today is a pleasant place to be. The sea lock still operates close to the museum and lifeboat house. Bude is a resort of some importance. Surfing is a major sport

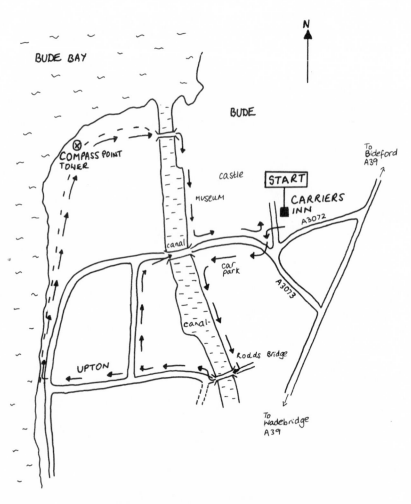

here, while the long sandy beaches are just made for the 'bucket and spade' brigade.

Conveniently situated, the Carriers is a busy pub, open all day throughout the year. A separate Steak and Salad Bar has a menu reflecting its location. Shark steak and crab salad are two dishes to be tried, while special vegetarian meals are also served. Fillet steak and prime rib can also be enjoyed in this attractive bar. The pub snacks are varied and tasty. Cornish pasty, barbecued bacon ribs or a pasta Napolitana are examples of what may be found on the 'Blackboard Specials' menu. The inn is known for its real ales, well-kept Courage Best and Directors being two popular ones. Fosters and Carlsberg lagers are on draught.

The opening times are from 11 am to 11 pm on weekdays throughout the year, with normal Sunday hours.

Telephone: 01288 352459.

How to get there: Bude lies off the A39 Bideford to Wadebridge road. Make for the town centre, turn right at the roundabout, go over a 'speed hump' and the pub is on your right.

Parking: There is some street parking close to the pub. A large public car park is nearby.

Length of the walk: 2 ½ miles. Map: OS Landranger 190 Bude and Clovelly (GR 210061).

There are few places where one can combine canal and coastal walking. The canal is a peaceful waterway bordering a nature reserve where one can spend a few minutes in a hide, watching the activity. A wide coastal path affords spectacular scenery over Widemouth and Bude Bays. This modern, bustling resort has a wealth of industrial archaeology, some of which has been incorporated in the walk. There is a well-maintained sea lock – quite a rarity – while a comprehensive museum and a castle are both adjacent to the canal. Seats and well-signed viewpoints along the way add to the pleasures of a very interesting route.

This pleasant stroll, with just one incline through the village of Upton, can happily be undertaken by most family groups. If you shorten the walk with a right turn through the village, back into Bude, you can easily take a pushchair.

The Walk

From the pub cross the road and turn left. At the T-junction turn right, over the bridge, cross over and walk diagonally through the car park to the footpath sign beside the canal. Turn left along the towpath. At the fork keep along the canal side. Bude Marshes nature reserve will be on your left, with the hide making a good place to spend some time looking across the meadow. Waterfowl and other birds who make their home in this marshy habitat are interesting to watch.

The RNLI boathouse, next to the sea lock.

From this point you quickly leave the built up area around Bude and enter a rural aspect. Benches are strategically placed and fishermen relax beside the peaceful waterway. Rodds Bridge will soon come into view. Cross the canal here and turn right, along a lane towards Upton village. There is a climb here as this narrow lane makes its way between the cottages. At a fork keep straight on, passing a few more cottages and ignoring the footpath sign on your right.

There is a lane just past here where buggy-pushers could walk back into Bude.

The village spreads along the top of the hill to a junction with the coast road, known as Upton Cross. Cross the road, carefully – it is particularly busy along here in the summer – to the signpost opposite, pointing left to Widemouth and right to Bude. Turn right along the coast path. Walk along a fenced track to a kissing-gate. Now cross a field. The satellite station on the skyline makes a landmark for miles around.

The path can be clearly seen over the next headland. Keep to the wide path rather than the one near to the fence on the cliffside. As I walked here, in late June, I had no hesitation in sitting on the conveniently placed seat to enjoy the song of the larks and the scent of clover all around me. Widemouth Bay stretches to your left, with its jagged cliffs bearing such rock formations of contorted strata that they attract people from all over the world.

Millook Haven is the place to drive to if you want to get nearer to these cliffs. But, be warned, the road is extremely steep and very narrow, to the access point.

From the trig point you can see Trevose Head beyond Padstow. The highest cliffs in Cornwall lie between here and that headland. From the viewpoint go through a kissing-gate and bear right, downhill, towards the town. However, it is well worth while to visit the small tower on your left. This is a 'Compass Point Tower' and a viewpoint.

Rejoin the wide track across the springy turf, leaving the coast path on your left. Bear left as you reach the bottom of the hill, through the gate, where you will see the sea lock and lifeboat house.

Turn right and walk over the lock bridge after passing the lifeboat. Turn right again, alongside the canal, noting the hand rails on your left. The museum is close by, where you will be able to absorb the fascinating industrial archaeology of this one-time port.

As you reach the road turn left and so back to the pub.

2 **Bolventor**
Jamaica Inn

Bolventor is a small moorland village. A church, a school and a few houses would scarcely have attracted more than a passing glance were it not for the world famous Jamaica Inn. Relatively peaceful once again as the A30 layout now bypasses the village, it is a good place to sample the delights of walking on the moors, with suitable refreshment at hand either before or after your exertion.

As you push open the huge wooden door and step onto the stone floor, trodden for centuries by the feet of hungry travellers, you may well forget the rows of modern cars and the fast moving traffic on the A30 which you have just left. Here is a hostelry, immortalised by Daphne du Maurier with her book of that name, which still retains that elusive quality of blending past and present. Percy the parrot, really a she, who has been here since 1953, occupies a place of honour in the bar and

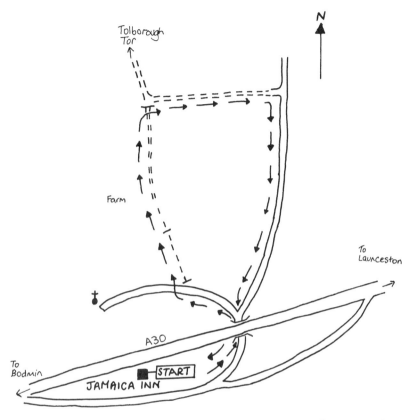

keeps visitors vastly amused with her repetition of some rather 'choice' words. The open fireplace, large enough to take the trunk of a small tree, has been here for 400 years. How many weary souls have warmed themselves at this ancient hearth? Blackened beams but comfortable furniture, low doorways but spacious dining areas, the old and the new exist contentedly together in this timeworn place. A moorland inn it still is, with Bodmin Moor brooding around it. Light and dark shadows play tricks with the imagination as you look across to the barren slopes of the tors about you. The highwayman, the smuggler, perhaps they too have enjoyed the hospitality and shelter that Jamaica Inn has to offer. It is now the turn of the 20th century traveller to partake of this fare.

A special entrance for children, with a family room, and

outdoor play area are recent additions. Mr Potter's Museum of Curiosity and the Daphne du Maurier room will keep many a restless youngster or nostalgic adult happily engaged for a while. A varied menu in the Pedlar's Food Bar or Merlyn's Restaurant takes care of the creature comforts. Who would not enjoy a 'Hot Proper Cornish Pasty' in such surroundings? Home-made pies are another choice and a 'Specials' blackboard describes the dishes of the day. Vegetarians are catered for with a modest selection of well-prepared food. A children's menu offers most of the favourites and is competitively priced. The restaurant serves both traditional and more exotic cuisine. Sesame seed toast and Japanese prawns or deep fried Camembert with redcurrant jelly are but two examples of delicious starters. A fillet steak or rack of lamb make good main courses. Real ales are served at Jamaica Inn – IPA, Cornish Original and Boddingtons. Newquay Steam on draught and Whitbread Best Bitter are other brews available. Guinness and Murphy's, along with a lager to your taste, a wine list and range of spirits should suit all who seek to quench their thirst.

The opening hours are 9 am to 9.30 pm for food and 11 am to 11 pm for drinks. The usual Sunday opening times apply for the bars.

Telephone: 01566 86250.

How to get there: Jamaica Inn lies just off the A30 between Launceston and Bodmin. It is well signposted from the main road.

Parking: There is plenty of parking space at the inn.

Length of the walk: 2 miles. Map: OS Landranger 201 Plymouth and Launceston area (GR 184768).

One might be forgiven for thinking that the intrusion of a dual carriageway so close to the moor would effectively spoil a short walk around Jamaica Inn. Not so. The paths remain unchanging, the rocks and clitter (debris) on the tors have not moved, while birds and animals still live their lives in the time honoured way. Nature adapts.

This walk explores moorland ways without venturing into the lonely stretches of land leading across to Brown Willy, which towers over the moor

14

Dozmary Pool – located south of the inn. (Woolf/Greenham Collection)

at a height of 1,375 ft. Farm tracks lead onto a quiet lane for the return route. Listen to the skylarks as they soar above you, and enjoy the feeling of isolation which moorland walking so often brings.

The Walk

From the pub car park turn left and then left again to pass under the bridge beneath the dual carriageway. Curving to the left, the road goes slightly downhill. Follow the signs for Bolventor church. On the brow of the hill, before going down to the church, look for a stile in the right-hand fence. Cross this, into a field, going over another stile and downhill towards the farm lying in the hollow below. Keep to the right of the farm and continue up the track towards the open moor.

Slightly uphill all the way, you will come to a five-barred wooden gate which is waymarked. Go through this and turn right along a wide track. On reaching the lane, turn to the right. This area is known as Tolborough, and Tolborough Tor will have been ahead of you as you walked the moor, rising to 1,113 ft. Continue walking along the lane, making your way back towards the pub and car park.

3 St Cleer
The Stag Inn

A truly moorland inn. Sheep and cattle wander along the unfenced roads on this part of the moor, which is registered as commonland. Reminders that this area of Cornwall has had settlers since the Bronze Age come with the archaeological sites of Trethevy Quoit and The Hurlers Stone Circles, near Minions. It was here that there was evidence of those strange little people who buried a metal beaker with their dead, hence 'Beaker Folk'. It is believed that St Cleer takes its name from a 7th century hermit called Clarus. He it was who founded a chapel, holy well and the nearby cross. During the mid 1800s St Cleer gained a degree of prosperity through the mining activities surrounding it. Many of the buildings in the community date from that time.

The Stag Inn lies at the entrance to the village, from the Liskeard direction. It is thought to have been built as an inn around 300 years ago. Unfortunately, the deeds were burnt during an air raid on Plymouth during the last war. This pleasant, welcoming place commands fine views across the moors. In the car park is a well, covered with a metal grid, while a private red telephone box stands proudly close by. An outdoor play area with suitable equipment should please the youngsters. A varied menu offers delicious bar meals – a Cornish pasty to satisfy even the most hungry walker, sandwiches and soup or a succulent steak served in generous portions by the friendly staff. Vegetarians can enjoy an omelette made with free range eggs, or a vegetable crumble. A speciality of the house is a six inch, deep pan pizza. Old fashioned puddings are served with custard or clotted cream. There is also a children's menu. High on the priority list at this inn are the well-kept real ales. Among these brews are Smiles Best Bitter, Hicks Special, Bass and West Country. Murphy's and Guinness, Carling, Carlsberg and Stella are also on draught. Inch's Stonehouse cider is a popular local drink.

The opening times are 11 am to 11 pm during the summer, and 12 noon to 3 pm, 7 pm to 11 pm during the winter. Normal Sunday opening hours apply.

Telephone: 01579 342305.

How to get there: St Cleer lies north of the Liskeard to Bodmin road, the A38. Travelling from Liskeard, take the Tavistock road. As you leave the town turn left, signed 'St Cleer'. In less than a mile turn left. The pub is on your right as you enter the village.

Parking: There is a large car park at the pub.

Length of the walk: 3 miles. Map: OS Landranger 201 Plymouth and Launceston area (GR 249679).

This pleasant, easy walk takes you through the lovely Rosecraddock Woods, across field paths and close to ancient farmsteads. The holy well and cross require a slight detour on the return route. Trethevy Quoit is signed from St Cleer and makes an interesting diversion. This is a chamber tomb of the megalithic period, the uprights and capstone having been covered in an earth mound.

17

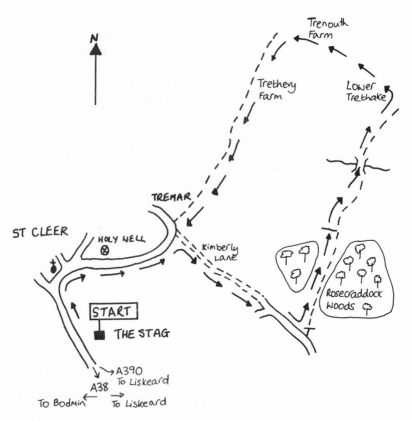

The Walk

From the pub turn right, down the road next to the church. Take the first turn right after passing the Market Inn. Continue down this road until you reach a crossroads. Turn left, proceed to a junction where there is a telephone box on your right and take the track, bearing right between the houses, known as Kimberly Lane. There is a white footprint mark on a post on your left. You will be following this sign throughout the walk. This area is known as Tremar Coombe.

Continue along the lane until you reach a road. Turn left. Walk for about 100 yards until you see a stile on your left and a waymark sign, into Rosecraddock Woods.

Follow the path through the woods until you reach a stile on your left, leading into a field. Keeping the hedge on your left,

18

The holy well at St Cleer.

cross diagonally to the stile in the corner. The path continues, diagonally towards a gate. Go through the gate and, keeping the hedge on your left, walk down to the footbridge which crosses the Seaton river. The path is now easy to follow through the fields until you reach a gate onto a road.

Turn left and walk past Trethake. This was a medieval manor. You may see mullioned windows in the cowshed, which was thought to have been a chapel. Continue along the road, through Trenouth farmyard. At the fork, turn left to Trethevy Farm. As you reach the farm, follow the white footprint signs around the buildings, up some steps and into a field. The path now crosses the field, diagonally to a kissing-gate. Once through this, follow the marker signs and footpath over the next three fields to a gate. Go through the gate onto the road back into Tremar and the start of Kimberly Lane. From here retrace your steps back up the road to the pub.

To see the holy well and cross, instead of turning left back to the Stag as you reach the church, walk down the hill for about 100 yards where you will see them on your right.

Places of interest nearby

You may like to complete your day in the area by visiting *Dobwalls Family Adventure Park* which is close by. Or, perhaps the *Carnglaze Slate Caverns*, between Dobwalls and St Neot. It was in these caverns that rum was stored during the last war. The sailors' 'ration' was distributed to the ships at Plymouth.

Kelly Bray
The Swingletree

It is believed that the name of this pub is unique. Known as the Railway Inn before the Beeching cuts of 1965 closed the local station, it then became the Swingletree. The pub sign depicts a shire horse pulling a plough. The swingletree is the piece of equipment hanging behind this massive animal which holds three whips. They would swing from a piece of wood and a chain. The landlord of the time happened to have this and other memorabilia of those farming days – so we have the 'Swingletree', obviously a corruption of 'swinging tree'.

A pub for over a century, an early photograph shows little change to this well-known Cornish inn. A large garden with picnic tables and chairs is a pleasant place to be on a sunny day. Barbecues are a feature during summer while the lounge and bar are comfortable and warm for other times. Children are welcome and there is a menu especially for them. The ploughman's lunch is hard to beat, as is the home-made steak and kidney pie. The 'Blackboard Special' is usually a generously

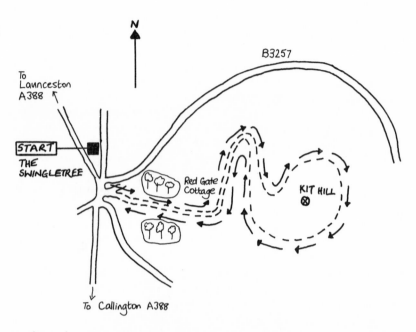

portioned meat and three veg. Jacket potatoes, sandwiches and salads are always available. Puddings include such delights as steamed sponge with chocolate sauce, while treacle pudding and clotted cream is a sure winner. A Courage house, well-kept real ales include Courage Best and Directors. John Smith's Keg is another popular beer. Fosters, Carlsberg and Kronenbourg are the lagers on draught.

The opening times are 11 am to 11pm on weekdays throughout the year, with normal Sunday hours. Food is available every day at lunchtime, from 11.30 am (Sunday 12.15 pm) to 2.30 pm (Saturday 11 am to 3 pm). In addition, the kitchen is open on Monday, Tuesday and Friday evenings from 5.30 pm to 9.30 pm and on Saturday from 4 pm to 9.30 pm.

Telephone: 01579 82395.

How to get there: Kelly Bray lies on the A388 Launceston to Callington road. The pub is in the centre of the village, just off the main road.

Parking: There is plenty of parking space at the pub.

Length of the walk: 2 ½ miles. Map: OS Landranger 201 Plymouth and Launceston area (GR 357718).

In a county renowned for its panoramas, Kit Hill is a magical place. The great moorland dome, bordered by the granites of Dartmoor and Bodmin Moor, rises to over 1,000 ft. Topped by an 85 ft stack, a relic of Kit Hill mine, it makes for fine walking on a clear day. This route has a gentle gradient on a firm track, pathways over moorland and the tall chimney which beckons you as you make your way towards it.

The Walk

Leave the car park, cross the minor road adjacent and walk towards the garage on your left. In a few yards you will see Florence Road on your left, signed 'Industrial Estate'. There is also a footpath sign. Proceed along this road through a car sales yard. As the road divides, bear right along a wide gravelled track. This climbs gently upwards through a wooded area. Notice the hanging mosses and lichen on the walls to your left. The incline levels out, passing Red Gate cottage then a large stone house on your right.

Continue ahead along the narrowing path, passing a barn on

A moorland scene with abandoned mine workings.

23

your right. At a fork, bear right following the blue arrow. You are now on the old horse trail used by horses and donkeys during the mining days of Kit Hill. Many small mining ventures scattered the whole area but were never successful on a large scale.

Pause at vantage points as you walk and look across to Caradon Hill with its tall radio mast. A patchwork of fields spreads out below you. At a blue marker sign take the path on the left to make for the tower. Keeping the large mine waste tip on your right, join a stone track. You can see the tower top from here. At the junction with a surfaced road, turn right.

At the top you will find two explicit viewpoints. The Tamar road bridge can be seen at Plymouth as can the Dartmoor landmarks of Sharptor and North Hessary Tor with its BBC TV mast. Walk around the outside perimeter of the earthwork. This dominant hill has been used for defensive purposes during many centuries. The battle of Hingston Down was fought just below here when the Saxons finally suppressed the Cornish. There is evidence that Kit Hill was probably an important stage in an overland tin route. As you walk round the earth bank notice the chimney stack below. Continue circling until you reach a green arrow post '6'. Mine tips and capped shafts are nearby. Take this path and walk on to the next green arrow number '7'. Do not take this signed path but the one to the left of it. At the fork keep left and continue until you reach a blue trail post. Turn right.

At the next fork and blue arrow sign do not follow the arrow but take the lower path. This will bring you back onto the horse trail and your original path and track down into Kelly Bray.

Places of interest nearby

Cotehele House (National Trust) on the banks of the river Tamar.

5 Cawsand
The Smugglers Inn

A delightful village in what is often called the 'Forgotten Corner' of Cornwall. Relatively close to Plymouth and with a coastline of wide sweeping beaches, dotted here and there with charming fishing villages, it is difficult to understand why this should be so. Just across the border from Devon and edged by the rivers Lynher and Tamar, Plymouth Sound and the sweep of Whitsand Bay, the Rame peninsula seems a haven of peace and tranquillity. Not so in days gone by. Notorious for smuggling, the pub in Cawsand is well named. Colourwashed cottages, flowers at every turn, narrow streets and spectacular walks make this historical fishing village a positive delight. One walk takes you over a field known as 'Hats and Bonnets'. High above the village, this would have been the church path to Forder. One can well imagine the traumas suffered when a high wind blew hats and bonnets away as families walked to church across the exposed hillside. This small village of Cawsand still contains a 'Shop in the Square', almost next to the pub.

The Smugglers began life in 1650 as two cottages. It then became a ship-chandler's before establishing itself as an inn almost 300 years ago. Smugglers' tunnels, now blocked, lead down to the shore. The bars have retained a look and atmosphere in keeping with their age and history. There are blackened beams and well-used seating. Walls are decorated with pictures and trophies which show the pub's association with its seafaring customers. A friendly, sociable pub, it prepares no set menu. Its daily specials will nearly always include local seafood such as scallops and crab. Local freshly caught fish is ever popular. However, beef in Guinness, a house speciality or a curry made by the landlord are all delicious. Vegetarian meals are prepared and served as required. Children are welcome. Although there is no special room for them, the dining area will, no doubt, keep them happily interested while they eat. Fish nets and pots, pictures and chat are such that I doubt whether they will miss the usual attributes of a family room. Real ales include Courage Best, Ruddles and a guest beer. Scrumpy Jack cider is a popular local drink. Three or four lagers and a full range of liqueurs and malt whiskies make this a well-stocked bar.

The opening times are 11.30 am to 4 pm and 7 pm to 11 pm during the period October to April, and 11 am to 11 pm in the summer. Food is available throughout the year from 12 noon to 2.30 pm and 7 pm to 9.30 pm. Sunday hours are 12 noon to 3 pm and 7 pm to 10.30 pm throughout the year.

Telephone: 01752 822309.

How to get there: From Torpoint take the A374 for Antony. Turn left at Antony and then on to the B3247 Mount Edgcumbe road. Leaving the B3247, take the unclassified road into Cawsand.

Parking: The pub does not have a car park. Leave your car, as you enter the village, in a large car park on your left. Walk down the path out of the car park towards the sea. The pub is on your left in the square.

Length of the walk: 3½ miles, or 4½ miles if you want to add a detour to the chapel on Rame Head. Map: OS Landranger 201 Plymouth and Launceston area (GR 435502).

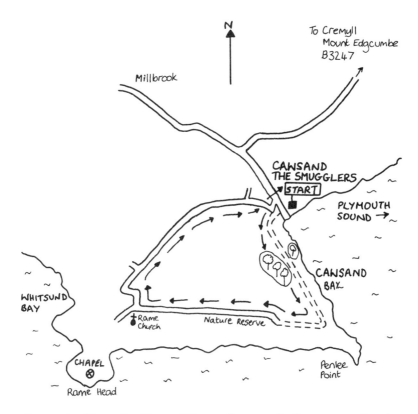

Cawsand and its twin village of Kingsand are on the Rame peninsula, close to Mount Edgcumbe Park. This walk includes some fine coastal scenery, a nature reserve and the ancient church at Rame. A military road, built during the 1939/45 war, cuts across the headland and makes for easy walking along this exposed area. A detour can be made onto Rame Head to the chapel which perches on top of the promontory. Sea birds cluster around the fishing boats as they enter Plymouth Sound, yet a woodland track as you begin the walk could be miles from any coastline. Easy walking for all family groups.

The Walk

From the pub walk back to the car park. Look to your left as you enter the car park where you will see a large Florentine-style house. Make for this and up some steps. Cross over the road, bearing right, and take the drive immediately on your left. This lovely wooded lane is almost a mile in length and a good

A gig crew prepares for a race.

20 minutes walk. It was built by an Earl Edgcumbe in the early 19th century as an access to Penlee Point. You will pass a flight of steps down to a coastguard station on your left.

As you leave the shady woodland drive the views explode before you, stretching from Devon to the Lizard. The Eddystone lighthouse is but ten miles away while Rame Head dominates the immediate skyline, with the chapel of St Michael standing proudly on the summit, a legacy of the past. A hermit priest lived in the upper part while services were held below.

Honeysuckle, scabious and valerian decorate this delightful area of Penlee Point. Bear right where there are numerous seats. As the track wends to the right go over a stile onto a footpath contained between two hedges. In about 300 yards look for a post with a black arrow and car park sign. This is easily missed, particularly while the vegetation is high, so look carefully. Turn right up some steps. Bear left after passing some iron railings, following the black arrow sign. Up some more steps, pass another bench on your right, go over a stile and continue into a car park. You are in a designated nature reserve. A notice will tell you of the species and varieties of plants and flowers to be found here.

Turn left out of the car park and join a narrow road. This is known as the Military Road and was built across fields for access to battlements during the Second World War. A pleasant walk, now, with wide-reaching views. As it ends, in approximately one mile, you will see Rame church on your left, the spire of which has been visible during your walk. This is believed to be the only church in the country still lit by candles and having a pump organ. There are memorials to many sailors in the churchyard.

It is from the church car park to your left that you can walk out onto Rame Head.

After a browse round the church turn right and take the road back to Cawsand. This road is very little used during the winter months. However, in summer there is some traffic so take care round the bends.

At the crossroads turn right down to the village and car park.

Places of interest nearby

While in this area of Cornwall why not visit *Mount Edgcumbe Country Park* or take the ferry across from Cremyll to Plymouth? Both give unsurpassed views of Plymouth Sound where naval ships and pleasure boats are always to be seen.

⑥ Crafthole
The Finnygook Inn

Most areas of the county can boast of smugglers and ghosts. The very name of this pub says it all. Gook is Cornish for ghost and Finny was the smuggler. Put the two together and one will quickly understand that Finny, killed nearby, haunts this old inn... Nobody admits to having seen him but legend dies hard.

Dating from the 16th century and set between the sea and countryside, the Finnygook presents a degree of luxury without losing out on the charm of these old premises. It is warm and comfortable and the friendly atmosphere extends to all comers. Children are welcome away from the bar area. Overnight accommodation is also available in well-appointed en suite rooms. There are separate bar and restaurant menus. I enjoyed a pasty of huge proportions, served in the bar – it was home-made and certainly had the required amount of meat, turnip, onion and potato. Sandwiches, salads and home-made soup of the day are all on the bar menu, with a selection of local fish dishes as available. Puddings are a speciality. The restaurant

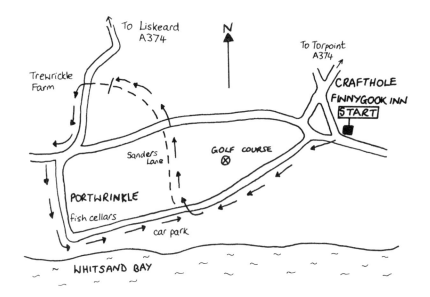

offers a wide and delectable choice of dishes to suit all tastes. Try fresh sea bass or a prime fillet steak. A freehouse, the Finnygook serves three real ales, which include Flowers Original, IPA and Wadworth 6X. Guinness and Murphy's are on draught. Heineken and Stella are the lagers, along with Newquay Steam and Tetley Yorkshire also on draught. An interesting wine list is available in both bar and restaurant.

The opening times are 11 am to 3 pm and 6 pm to 11 pm on Monday to Saturday, with normal Sunday hours.

Telephone: 01503 30338.

How to get there: From Torpoint take the A374. Crafthole lies south of Sheviock and is signed from the A374.

Parking: There is parking at the pub and a public car park by the beach in Portwrinkle, ½ mile away, down the hill from Crafthole. You may prefer to start the route from there and walk to the pub.

Length of the walk: 2½ miles. Map: OS Landranger 201 Plymouth and Launceston area (GR 366542).

A culver-house or dovecote that can be viewed along the route.

Walk the old sand route used by donkeys to transport beach sand for sweetening the inland acid fields. Quiet, shady lanes and the coastpath at Portwrinkle all combine to make this pleasant stroll one to be remembered.

The Walk

If you start from the pub, walk down the lane opposite, passing the golf course on your right. Look across the course where you should be able to see a 'culver house' or dovecote. It pre-dates the golf course by at least five centuries, being built during the 14th century.

At the bottom of the hill look for a footpath sign on your right. Follow this into the golf club car park. Walk through the first parking area, ignoring the wooden steps on your right, and continue into the upper part. Here you will see some stone steps in the right-hand corner. Go up these and into Sanders Lane. You are now on the sand trail. Lane it may have been at one time but it is a not very wide footpath today. However, it is a delightful, shady place with wind shaped trees and tall plants. On reaching a lane, go across and continue over the stile to the second part of Sanders Lane. You will emerge onto another lane. Turn left. This is Trewickle Lane, really more of a farm road with very little traffic. Pass Trewickle Farm on your right as you climb the hill. Records show that a farm has been on this site for over 800 years.

Continue until you reach the coast road. This is busy in the summer, so do be careful as you cross. Turn right. A mown grass verge is left for you to walk on. In a few yards turn left down a very steep hill. This is Donkey Lane. One can well imagine the donkeys struggling up here with loaded panniers on each side. Fortunately you are walking down...

As you reach the bottom of the hill and the old harbour area look to your left. Here are the remains of the fish cellars. These were a hive of industry until the middle of the 19th century when the pilchards moved away and left many villages along this coast deprived of a living. The huge catches of pilchards were brought into the tiny harbour, where they were unloaded, taken to the cellars and packed into barrels between layers of salt. Many were exported to Latin countries where they would be eaten during Lent. The associated industries of coopering and fertiliser making, with the waste products, were activities closely associated with the cellars. One can well imagine the total devastation when this livelihood was taken away.

Walk along the sea front and up the hill to return to the pub.

Places of interest nearby

The nearby National Trust property of *Antony House* is a good place to visit and close to Crafthole. Built between 1710 and 1721 it is still lived in by members of the Carew-Pole family. It has a lovely garden and the house is open to the public on a guided tour basis. It lies 2 miles from Torpoint off the A38. Opening times: 1st April – end October, Tuesdays, Wednesdays, Thursdays and Bank Holiday Mondays 1.30 pm – 5.30 pm. Also Sundays in June, July and August.

Lerryn
The Ship Inn

The wooded banks of the Lerryn river, which joins the Fowey above Golant, make a perfect setting for this village of pretty cottages. Boats pull on their moorings as the river rushes in on a high tide and are then left high and dry as it recedes. Ducks there are in plenty. The car park, beside the river, must be a duck's paradise as picnickers dispose of unwanted crusts to the eagerly waiting webbed foot families. Summer evenings see boat trips up from Fowey. As visitors enjoy their supper the captain keeps a wary eye on the state of the tide.

This delightful riverside pub originated in the 17th century as three small cottages and a butcher's shop. However, for the last 200 years it has served food and drink to folk travelling by both river and road. Local farm cider was brewed here, while the cellar of today was the slaughterhouse of yesterday. Tythes for the vast Rashleigh Estates were brought to this inn, always, as it is now, the centre of village life. Children are welcome here, with plenty of room away from the bar area. A garden equipped

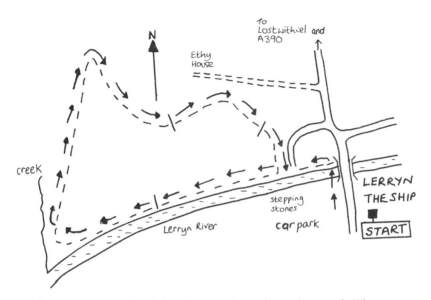

with swings and climbing frames is at their disposal. The menu is comprehensive. It offers such dishes as Fowey sea trout, local lemon sole, and steak and oyster pie. Pheasant and cranberry or venison pie are two favourites. The vegetarian has a good choice. Country lentil crumble and mushroom and nut fettuccine are but two of the dishes. Sweets are traditional and a children's menu offers most of the favourites at competitive prices. Four real ales are kept: Courage Best Bitter, Bass, Ruddles County and Otter Ale, the latter from a local brewery. Worthington and Toby, Tennents Extra, Fosters Draught and a local scrumpy are included in the list.

The opening times are 11.30 am to 3 pm and 6 pm to 11 pm. Food is served from 12 noon to 2.30 pm and 7 pm to 9.30 pm, and on Sunday between 12.30 pm and 2 pm and 7.30 pm and 9.30 pm.

Telephone: 01208 872374.

How to get there: From St Austell take the A390 Liskeard road and after Lostwithiel, look for a sign on the right for Lerryn. Alternatively, go through Lostwithiel, turning right at the pedestrian lights. Turn right at the river bridge, over the railway level crossing and right at the next turn for Lerryn.

The Lerryn river.

Parking: A public car park (free) is adjacent to the inn.

Length of the walk: 2 ½ miles. Map: OS Landranger 200 Newquay and Bodmin (GR 141569).

Part woodland, part field walking, with peaceful river scenes, this circuit is suitable for all ages. The mansion, Ethy House, surrounded by rhododendrons in the spring, surveys the parkland through which you walk.

The Walk

From the pub walk across the car park towards the river. Stepping stones at low tide! If you don't fancy those then walk through a gap between the toilets and the village hall and along the lane to the bridge. Go over the bridge and turn left just above the river. Continue until you reach the stepping stones. Walk on alongside the river (turning left if you used the stones).

As the road ends pass behind a house and into Ethy Woods (NT). Keep straight on, following the river. Ignore wooden steps on your right. Rhododendrons make a colourful show here in early summer. At the marker sign walk straight on, leaving the river. In a few yards, at the fork, bear right between wooden posts. These are beautiful mixed woods, a carpet of leaves with ferns and mosses forming decorations on the fallen tree trunks.

Keep on the grassy track straight ahead. At the next junction turn right. You will be turning back on yourself, but higher in the wood. Go slightly uphill here for about 200 yards until you see a stile into a field and a footpath arrow. Ethy House, privately owned, will be on your left as you walk across the field. Continue diagonally, towards a netted coppice, keeping it on your right. A footpath sign on the end of the fencing directs you towards a gap, visible ahead. Go through this into the adjacent field.

Bear left now, keeping the wire fence on your left, to the next visible stile. Follow the footpath sign diagonally across the field towards the end of the houses and the beginning of the wood. There is another stile here. Walk between the wood and the garden into a close of houses. Turn left. Keep on the main drive to the road. Turn right. This will take you back down to the river, where you can return to the pub via the stepping stones or the bridge.

Places of interest nearby

The lovely old town of Lostwithiel is well worth a visit, as is *Restormel Castle* (English Heritage) 1½ miles to the north.

8 Fowey
The Ship Inn

It is almost impossible to write a brief description of Fowey. This small town, among many in Cornwall, has a history as exciting as any in Britain. From the Norman Conquest to the 20th century there is scarcely a decade that does not present us with illustrious deeds and happenings. Pronounced 'foy' to rhyme with 'joy', it can boast of authors such as Sir Arthur Quiller-Couch, known as 'Q', with his wonderful story of *Troy Town*, and Daphne du Maurier, whose home overlooked the ferry from Bodinnick. Each and every one of these people brought fame to this small town, so aptly described by James Barrie when he wrote 'It is but a toy town to look at, on a bay so small, hemmed in so picturesquely by cliffs and ruins that of a moonlight night it might pass for a scene in a theatre.' How right he was.

The Treffry family of Place House, that magnificent, turreted building behind the church, were closely associated with the Rashleighs, another prominent Cornish family. It was the Rashleighs, cousins of Sir Francis Drake, who lived in the Ship Inn during the 16th century. Seventy men from the town manned his ship *Frances of Fowey*. The Ship Inn was so named to preserve the name of this gallant little vessel. Of course the inn has altered over the centuries but the front of the building remains the same as it did 200 years ago. Centrally situated, the Ship is close to the town quay. Do look at the fine stained glass window at the inn. Dating from about 1880, it was made by the glass-making firm of Clayton and Bell.

A St Austell Brewery house, it serves a good pint of draught real ale. Most of the popular lagers and ciders are available. House wine by glass or bottle is competitively priced. Children are not allowed in the bar but a family room caters for their needs and there is a special menu for them to choose their favourite meals. A lively, busy pub, the Ship offers a good variety of dishes. Five 'Specials of the Day' vary according to season, while a full fish menu makes good use of local catches. Home-made soup, steak pasties or a crab salad make tasty snacks. A choice of sweets to whet the appetite are served in generous helpings with clotted cream.

The opening times are 11 am to 3 pm and 6 pm to 11 pm October to April, and 11 am to 11 pm in the summer. Sunday hours are 12 noon to 3 pm and 7 pm to 10.30 pm (all year). Food is served 12 noon to 2.30 pm and 6 pm to 9 pm (all year).

Telephone: 01726 833751.

How to get there: Fowey can be reached from the A390 St Austell to Bodmin road and is signposted from St Blazey. To park in Caffa Mill car park take the sign for 'The Docks'. The walk is described from this point.

Parking: It is not possible to park in the centre of Fowey during the summer months. Leave your car either at Caffa Mill car park near the docks and walk through the town or at the Top car park when you will walk down many steps to the centre of the town. There is a car park at the harbour where you might be lucky to find a space.

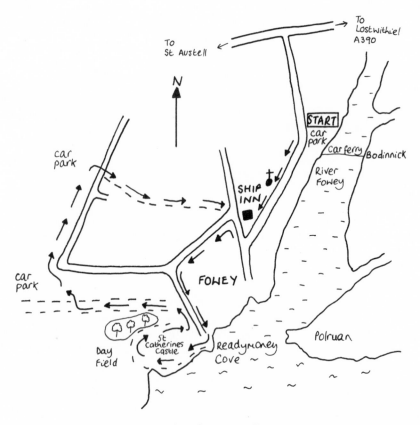

Length of the walk: 3 miles from Caffa Mill car park, 2 miles from the pub. Map: OS Landranger 200 Newquay and Bodmin (GR 125516).

A walk steeped in history combined with unsurpassed views of the Fowey estuary. Watch the boats, the people, the birds. Enjoy the narrow straggling streets, colour-washed cottages and flowers. There is some uphill walking to St Catherine's Point. This is, without doubt, the best vantage point for views of Polruan, Fowey and the estuary. Photographers will love it.

The Walk
From the car park, head south along the narrow street running parallel with the river. You will, no doubt, have spent a few minutes watching the car ferry to Bodinnick load and unload

and the ships taking out china clay brought here from the pits at St Austell.

Pass the town houses, tall and colourful, the craft shops and ship-chandlers as you squeeze your way along the increasingly narrow street. The custom house and Harbour Master's office make one fully aware that Fowey is not just a holiday town but a very important port even today.

As you reach the church and Ship Inn I am sure you will have difficulty in passing some of the fascinating little shops that line the streets. I always have to 'just pop in'. After leaving the Ship on your right continue uphill to the first turn left. Ignore paths leading to the water. After passing the Fowey Hotel keep straight on. You will have a good view of Polruan and the ferry from here. At a junction go straight on. At the next junction take the lower road, leading down to Readymoney Cove. It was given this name because of the many underwater artefacts beached here when divers had been exploring around the wrecks in this area.

Cross the beach if the tide is low, to a flight of steps leading into the wood. If the tide is high, then walk round the beach up a track and into the woods. Keep on the main pathway.

The view from St Catherine's Castle across to Polruan.

You will arrive at a junction of paths. Take the lower one towards St Catherine's Castle – a small artillery fort believed to have been built during the early part of the reign of Henry VIII to protect Fowey Haven. Below the fort is a two-gun battery of 1855.

Retrace your steps up the path. Take the lower path at the fork, passing a bench in a recess. Turn left and you will now have views out to sea. At the junction turn right.

The coastal path goes left through a gate into a field, given to the people of Fowey by Mr and Mrs Allday and known as the Day Field. It is not really on your route but is a good place to relax before continuing your walk.

Having turned right, pass some posts on your left and go straight on to the main track, ignoring steps on your left. Turn left and follow the track downhill. The bedrock here is slate and can be slippery if wet. Bend right at the bottom of the track back to Readymoney Beach. Walk back up the lane. At the first junction, opposite iron gates, turn left into Readymoney Copse (National Trust), up St Catharine's Parade. This is a pleasant tree-lined walk. In about 300 yards look for an exit on your right where there are metal hand rails. This leads into a car park. Cross the car park to the road and turn left. You are now in Hanson Drive. Cross over Gallant Drive. There are benches along here on which to sit and enjoy the view across to Pont Pill on the other side of the river. Pass the entrance to Fowey Hall on your left. Just opposite the car park entrance turn right, taking the 'Town Centre' sign. You now have many steps to negotiate until you reach a road. Turn right. You will be able to see Place House as you walk down here, just behind the church. Retrace your steps back to the pub and the car park.

Places of interest nearby

A day in Fowey would not be complete without a boat trip up river, tide permitting, or a cruise around the estuary if it is low water. Visit the *Museum*, opposite the Ship Inn, or take the foot ferry over to Polruan. All or any of these will make your visit to Fowey even more memorable.

Gorran Haven
The Llawnroc Hotel and Inn

A sheltered fishing village, Gorran Haven is right on the coastal footpath. Much of the coastline here is in the care of the National Trust, including Dodman Point with its stupendous views to the mouth of the river Fal. There are many secluded spots for the sea angler, while others prefer to watch the fishing boats unload their catch at the harbour. An old lime kiln still retains its place in the village. The acid soil of the county needed lime to sweeten it. Before the days of modern fertilisers ships would bring limestone into the villages, where it would be burned in the kilns before being ready to spread on the fields.

It is fortunate that a 'village battle' was resolved when, in 1961, the courts granted a licence to the Llawnroc. A club before that time, it has blossomed into a friendly, well appointed hotel and inn, popular with locals and visitors. It is itself a picturesque building and overlooks the lovely village and bay. There is a garden equipped with suitable chairs and tables for summer eating and drinking and, inside, the spacious

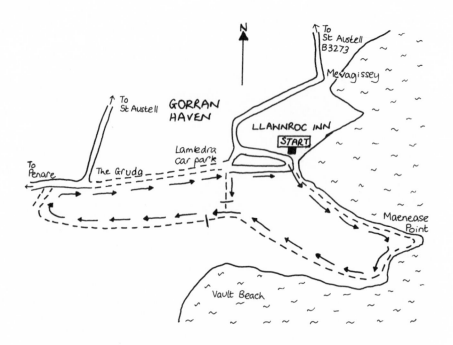

lounges have views of Gorran. The varied menu should provide something to suit everyone. There is always a vegetarian 'Dish of the Day' along with other 'Blackboard Specials'. A local home-made pasty is delicious and very filling. Sandwiches, jacket potatoes or a home-made soup are other lunchtime bar snacks. Evening meals include fresh whole lemon sole or a choice of steaks. Children have a menu of their own which also includes a vegetarian dish. Three real ales (usually IPA, Old Speckled Hen and Wadworth 6X) are pumped at the well-stocked bar. A family room is available and children are made to feel very welcome.

The opening times are 12 noon to 2.30 pm and 7 pm to 11 pm from October to April and 11 am to 3 pm and 6 pm to 11 pm in the summer. Sunday hours throughout the year are 12 noon to 3 pm and 7 pm to 10.30 pm. Food is served (throughout the year) from 12 noon to 2 pm and 7 pm to 9.30 pm.

Telephone: 01726 843461.

How to get there: From St Austell take the B3273, signed 'Mevagissey'. During the summer months it is best to avoid driving through Mevagissey. Take the road, signed 'Gorran', to the right at the top of the hill outside Pentewan. Continue past the village of Gorran and take a right turn, signed 'Gorran Haven'. Go down Bell Hill and turn left when you reach a grass triangle with a telephone box. Follow the 'coastguard' signpost. Keep straight on until you reach the inn on your left.

Parking: There is a good car park at the pub.

Length of the walk: 3½ miles (2½ if using Lamledra car park). Map: OS Landranger 204 Truro, Falmouth and surrounding area (GR 013415).

This walk will give you some of the most breathtaking scenery of the south coast. Walk above Vault Beach towards the Dodman, which stretches ahead. Use an old military road known as the Gruda.

If you prefer to avoid the initial stretch of coastal path, which has some steep places, drive your car to Lamledra car park and walk the circular walk from there. The landlord of the Llawnroc will point you in the right direction.

The Walk
From the pub, turn left, downhill to the village centre. This is a typical Cornish steep hill with pink and white painted cottages and a variety of hanging baskets – Chute Lane – it is well named. Turn right at the beach. The lime kiln is on your left.

Turn left before reaching the fish and chip shop. There is a footpath sign pointing along the coastal path to 'Vault Beach ½ mile'. Follow the signed path. Some cliff strengthening was going on when I was there so the route was diverted slightly. As you progress along the path you will be entertained by numerous sea birds. I saw cormorant, shag and a whole colony of kittiwake with their nesting places on the steep cliffs below the point. Sea anglers find this a good spot to cast their lines. I doubt if it really matters about the catch, just being there is enough . . .

Keep to the lower path as you round the headland. The higher one, a short cut, is rather a scramble. The path now widens and the walking is easy, although slightly uphill once

Coastal scenery above Vault beach.

you are past the point. Keep right when you reach the acorn
sign. Vault Beach lies below you. Go through the gate (there is
a bench here if you need it) and continue to follow the wide
grassy path towards Lamledra House on your right. Make for the
memorial seat.

The shortened version of the walk joins the route here. Having left
the car park by the steps, sea side, onto the coastal path, climb
a stile and reach the memorial seat.

Take the path through a wooden gate into a field. The width
of the path and easy walking conspire to make your apprecia-
tion of the magnificent views complete. At a signpost and cross-
track turn right for 'Penare ⅓ mile'. This is a delightful track.
At the lane turn right, then continue to the next junction and
turn right again.

This narrow lane is the start of the old military road, installed
during the 1939/45 war. It is a gated road and you will soon
reach the first gate. Continue along this tarmacked lane until
you reach Lamledra car park. Keep on the lane, now very
narrow but with little traffic, until you come to Foxall Lane.

Turn right here and so return to the village.

By the way – in case you haven't noticed – Llawnroc is Cornwall backwards!

Places of interest nearby

The Victorian garden, known as *Heligan*, lies between Gorran and Mevagissey.

⑩ Malpas
The Heron Inn

Set at the meeting point of three waterways, the Heron commands views to capture the imagination of even the most prosaic amongst us. The Tresillian and Truro rivers join with the Fal and make their way down to the sea at Falmouth. A ferry and inn certainly stood here in 1774 when a lease was granted by Viscount Falmouth of Tregothnan. Today, the ferry operates between Truro and Falmouth, using Malpas as a starting point at low tide. This is a pleasant trip, passing the King Harry Ferry before reaching the wide, deep waters of Falmouth harbour. Originally known as the Park Inn, the pub now takes its name from the heronry established in Kea Woods, just opposite, since the 1940s. Herons are part of the scenery here and one would be very unlucky to miss seeing the statue-like birds keeping watch for their supper.

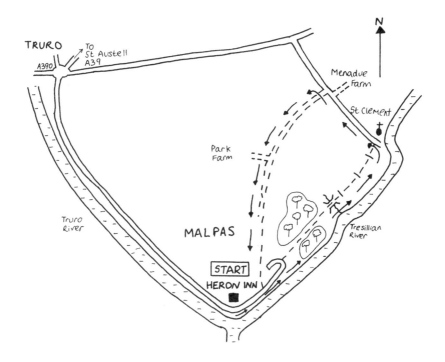

The Heron has a dining area and a long lounge bar looking out on to the river. It is comfortably furnished with some outside seating for the summer days. Children are welcome away from the bar area and have their own menu. Light meals include large filled rolls with salad, local smoked trout or a vegetable stroganoff with granary roll and butter. Evening grills are popular, with a mixed grill topping the list. The display of puddings is enough to tempt the strongest-willed – and they are all served with clotted cream if required. Cream teas are served during the summer months. A St Austell house, the two real ales are Tinners and Hicks Special. Scrumpy Jack, Guinness and two lagers are on draught. A comprehensive wine list is also available.

In summer the pub is open from 11 am to 11 pm on Monday to Saturday, and in winter the hours are 11 am to 2.30 pm and 6.30 pm to 11 pm. Normal Sunday opening times apply.

Telephone: 01872 72773.

Truro Cathedral. (Woolf/Greenham Collection)

How to get there: Malpas is reached from the A39 Falmouth to St Austell road and is signposted from the roundabout to the south of Truro city centre. Follow the Malpas road as far as the Heron, on the left.

Parking: There is a small car park at the Heron but cars can also be parked along the road on the approach to the pub.

Length of the walk: 3 miles. Map: OS Landranger 204 Truro, Falmouth and surrounding area (GR 842427).

A walk combining river bank, woods and farmland. This sheltered corner of Cornwall boasts a host of wild flowers, shrubs and plants. Visit the church at St Clement and enjoy the field paths between the two villages. A pleasant, easy walk suitable for most family groups.

The Walk
From the pub turn left down the lane towards the ferry. Notice a row of figureheads on the roof of a garage. Continue along the lane as far as you can go, to where there is a footpath sign on the right to 'St Clement'. Take this path through woodland, well signed and easy to follow. Pass through a kissing-gate, following the arrow down some steps and over a stream. Now pass through a rather strange metal gate into a field. Turn left and then follow a well worn path uphill towards a row of trees at the top of the hill. Now go through the iron kissing-gate and follow the path along the left-hand hedge. Turn left at the end of the field, with a footpath sign and iron gate into the next field.

On reaching the lane turn left to continue the walk, but turn right to look at the church. The slight detour is very rewarding. It was here that a former Bishop of Bombay lived and there are memorials to him in the church. To explore a little further, take the lane going beside the churchyard, downhill. You will come to a small beach area beside the Tresillian river.

To resume the walk, having turned left onto the lane, continue uphill for about ¼ mile. Just past Menadews Farm look for a narrow lane on your left, signed 'Park Farm'. Take this road and continue along it until the tarmac finishes and it becomes a track. As the track ends, walk straight ahead through a wooden gate into an enclosed path. There are no signs here but it is well walked. Go through another wooden gate. You can see the Tresillian river below. Take the left-hand path as you enter the wood, down a long flight of shallow wooden-edged steps to the lane. Turn right and so back to the pub.

Places of interest nearby

Truro museum and cathedral are both worth a visit. A collection of Cornish minerals in the museum reflect the mining era of this county.

11 Manaccan
The New Inn

The New Inn has a history dating back to the 16th century. Stories of smugglers and underground passages can be heard in this village, situated so close to Gillan creek, where the Helford river empties into Falmouth Bay. Despite being close to the high ridge of Goonhilly Downs (and the Earth Satellite Station), this area of Cornwall, known as the Meneage district, is so sheltered that rare and beautiful plants thrive in abundance. Tranquil creeks delight the walker. Boats are safely moored and children play on the stony beaches looking for crabs and cockles. Manaccan church is noted for the fig tree which grows from the wall. It is thought that a seed was dropped into the masonry, flourished and produced this well-grown tree. I know of one other such tree, growing from the porch wall of the church at St Newlyn East, near Newquay.

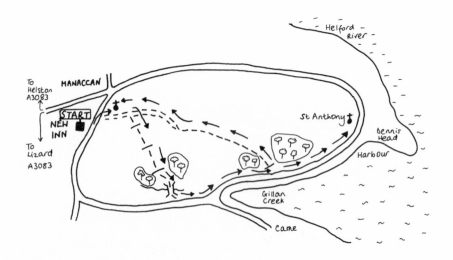

The traditional decor of an inn situated in a location such as this has been maintained by Greenalls brewery. Old settles and chairs match the oak beams overhead. Children can sit away from the bar while locals will regale the visitor with village news. Real ales, drawn from barrels, provide a good pint. The usual lagers are served and a range of wines and spirits.

There is no set menu. Instead a daily 'Blackboard' rings the changes, which include many dishes prepared from local produce. Children are offered smaller portions. A large flower-bordered garden is a peaceful setting in which to enjoy your meal during the summer months.

The opening times are 11 am to 3 pm and 6 pm to 11 pm on Monday to Saturday, with the usual Sunday hours.

Telephone: 01326 231323.

How to get there: From Helston take the A3083, signed 'The Lizard'. After passing through Culdrose Naval Air Station, turn left at a roundabout, signed 'Mawgan' and 'St Keverne'. Turn left again in about one mile, signed 'Mawgan' and follow the lanes to Manaccan.

Parking: Parking at the pub is rather limited. Park, neatly, in the village.

54

Length of the walk: 2 miles, or 3½ miles if you add a detour to St Anthony in Meneage. Map: OS Landranger 204 Truro, Falmouth and surrounding area (GR 764250).

A pleasant amble through field paths and quiet lanes. The woodland and creekside walking offers the opportunity to see unusual flowers and ferns. Attractive cottages in isolated places may well be a city dweller's idea of heaven ... at least in the summer.

The detour into St Anthony will add 1½ miles . The lane alongside Gillan creek provides level walking. Here you will find a ship-chandler's and boats pulled up onto the stony shore beside the church.

The Walk

Leave the pub and walk towards the church. Go through the churchyard, where you will see the fig tree. Proceed through the gate and into the lane opposite and walk straight ahead following the direction of the footpath sign.

In about 100 yards look for a footpath sign on your right, signed 'Carne'. Go down this track. Cross the stile into a field. Keeping the hedge on your right and following the well-defined path, make for another stile, leading into a coppice. Go over the next stile and follow the well-worn path as the wood thickens.

Descend to the accompaniment of the sound of running water from the stream on your right. The path wends down to a bridge, a really lovely spot, and out onto a lane. Turn left. In about 200 yards you will reach a junction. Take the signposted lane to 'St Anthony, 1 mile'. You now begin to walk along Gillan creek. This narrow road is used rarely in the winter and even summer traffic is very light. In about ¼ mile look for a wooden gate on your left with a footpath sign to Manaccan.

This is where you will make the detour to St Anthony if you so wish. The church is the focal point of the hamlet, with a tower built from stone brought from France. The story goes that a group of sailors from Normandy transported the stone and erected the tower as a thanksgiving for being saved during a storm. An ancient whipping post stands just inside the entrance gate and there are tombstones with some quite fantastic verses. After soaking up the atmosphere, retrace your steps to the wooden gate and 'Manaccan' sign.

Go through the gate onto a woodland track which soon

Satellite dishes at Goonhilly.

narrows. You may encounter a muddy place here during wet weather. Maybe you will be lucky enough to emerge from the shadows of the wood, as I did, into brilliant sunlight with a bed of shining white lilies on your right.

Join a green track, passing between some cottages and go on to a concrete driveway. At the top of the incline keep straight on. Ignore the footpath sign on your right. This wide track continues until you reach the lane from which you began the walk.

Instead of returning to the pub via the churchyard, bear left, past the post office, to the well. Now closed up, it makes an interesting and decorative piece of local history.

Places of interest nearby

The Seal Sanctuary at Gweek is situated on the Helford river about 7 miles from Manaccan. Injured and sick seals are cared for here and then returned to the wild.

Flambards Village at Helston is a theme park which attracts all age groups. Approached, from Manaccan, through the *Naval Air Station* at Culdrose – a stop can be made here at the viewing area.

56

12 Lizard village
The Top House

Originally a farmhouse, this popular inn became a licensed hostelry about 200 years ago. Set in the centre of the village, it is a good place from which to explore the paths and tracks to the most southerly point of the British Isles. The Lizard peninsula, with its acres of open moorland and natural beauty is, surprisingly enough, host to one of the most complex establishments of communications technology in the world. Goonhilly Satellite Earth Station dominates the landscape, yet in no way detracts from the wild beauty of the coast and moor. In the area above Kynance Cove the rare Cornish heath flourishes (*Erica Vagans*). Serpentine, one of the oldest of rocks, is quarried here and craftsmen work at producing lighthouses, ashtrays and other ornaments, watched by interested visitors.

The Top House boasts beer pump handles and ashtrays made from serpentine, while some of the bar furniture has seen a more hazardous life in ships' cabins. The large bar is usually full of tourists and locals. Many of the village men have a part to play at the lifeboat station just down the road. Most are fishermen and enjoy a chat about their experiences. The food is

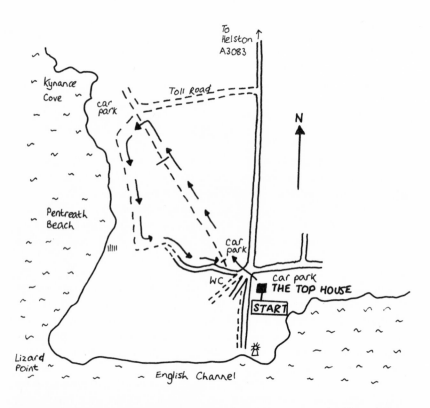

traditional and good. Home-made soup is a popular lunchtime snack, as is the more filling pasty. Other possibilities are fresh crab sandwiches, smoked mackerel salad or a 'Seafarer's Plate' which includes crab, prawns, mussels, cockles, smoked salmon and mackerel and gives pleasure to even the most jaded palate. A vegetarian and vegan menu is available. Children are welcome at this pub, which caters for them with their own menu. Puddings are ever popular and the variety here is well known. Three hand-pumped real ales are Marston's Pedigree, Cornish Original and Flowers IPA. Lagers and ciders, Guinness and Murphy's are complemented by an excellent wine list. Ten malt whiskies are cherished by the landlord.

In high summer the pub is open from 11 am to 11 pm. In winter the hours are 11 am to 3 pm and 6 pm to 11 pm. The usual Sunday times apply throughout the year.

Telephone: 01326 290456.

How to get there: From Helston take the A3083 signed 'The Lizard'.

Parking: A free public car park is adjacent to the pub.

Length of the walk: 2½ miles. Map: OS Landranger 203 Land's End and The Lizard (GR 703126).

This walk explores the field and coastal paths around Lizard village. Look for rare plants and enjoy the contrast of the lovely blue squill and pink thrift if you walk this way in the spring. Snipe and mallard occasionally rest on the wet ditches. These are easy-to-follow paths with the novelty of walking along a Cornish hedge, yes really . . . You may also wish to visit the lighthouse (check opening times in the village) or make a detour into Kynance Cove.

The Walk
From the car park pass in front of the public toilets towards a house called Rocklands. Take the first right-hand track to a footpath sign behind a small white building. Go up some rough steps onto a path along a Cornish hedge. A Cornish hedge is a substantial object – stone walls are infilled with soil and turfed over, making a wide top.

After crossing the field in this way go down some steps into a spinney. The path then goes up and down some more steps and over a step stile. Now cross another field to a further stile, which takes you to a lane leading down into Kynance Cove. Detour here if you like as there is a National Trust shop and toilets, as well as the magnificent rock formations of the famous bay.

To continue the walk without the detour, turn left for a few yards and take the first path on your left, through heather, and proceed down the track towards the sea. Views across the bay are superb. One third of the world's shipping passes Lizard Point and you would be very unlucky not to see some of the larger container ships passing by, as well as fishing boats and trawlers.

Go through a small car park, with a white house on your right. Walk on for about 20 yards until you reach the coastal path. Turn left. The path is wide here and well away from the cliff edge. As you make your way along the coast you will climb some 'interesting' stiles, passing over one into a field and back again, onto the coastal path.

Continue walking until you pass behind a rocky outcrop and reach a stream with steps and bridge. Do not go over the bridge but turn left along a well-worn path. This soon reaches a stile and a small coppice. There are footpath signs en route. The path widens out into a track on reaching a house. Follow the track until you reach the lane you started from, with the car park and pub ahead.

Places of interest nearby

Take the opportunity to visit the *Lizard lighthouse*. It is now possible to walk comfortably down a relatively new path to Lizard Head and probably easier than driving. It is signed from Lizard village. The lighthouse is open to the public at most times, other than when there is a gale or thick fog.

13 Porthleven
The Harbour Inn

In the 18th century Porthleven was known as Port Elvan and had a small population wresting a living from fishing, farming and mining. In 1811 a harbour was constructed and by 1848 there were 63 fishing boats engaged in the industry. Recorded catches show a variety of heavy weights. A crab weighed in at 12 lb, lobsters at 9 lb and 10 lb, with possibly the most exciting catch in 1983, when a royal sturgeon tipped the scales at 6 stone. This majestic fish fetched £2,018.25 at Newlyn auction and finished up on the table at the Grosvenor House Hotel in London. Porthleven still accommodates a number of fishing boats, along with pleasure craft whose crews use this delightful harbour from which to explore the south coast.

The Harbour Inn has a long history. Known as The Commercial before the harbour was built, it still retains tethering loops for horses. It has been sympathetically adapted to modern day needs and is welcoming and friendly. An attractive dining room offers a range of tasty dishes. Moules marinière,

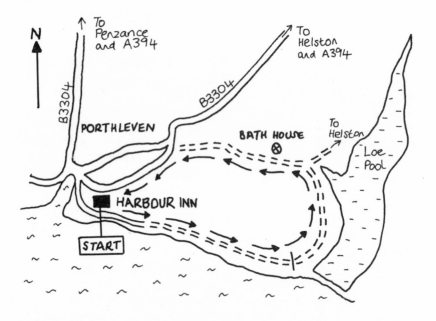

clam frit Marie Rose and king prawns in garlic butter are typical local specialities. Dover or lemon sole, plaice and monkfish also appear on the well-presented menu. From the grill, a fillet or entrecôte steak make a succulent dish for the hungry. Sandwiches and ploughman's lunches, children's favourites and a selection of sweets complete the menu. Children are welcome, away from the bar area, in the spacious rooms over-looking the harbour. The well-kept real ales include Hicks Special Draught (OG 1049-1053), Bosun's Keg, Duchy, Wreckers and XXXX mild. Carlsberg, Guinness and Strongbow are all on draught. Wines from France and Germany are served by the glass or bottle.

The opening times are 11 am to 11 pm on Monday to Saturday throughout the year. Normal Sunday hours apply, 12 noon to 3 pm and 7.30 pm to 10.30 pm.

Telephone: 01326 573876.

How to get there: Porthleven is south-west of Helston, on the B3304.

62

Parking: Follow the signs and turn left as you approach the harbour. There is limited parking along the harbour wall opposite the pub.

Length of the walk: 3 miles. Map: OS Landranger 203 Land's End and The Lizard (GR 615255).

This is an exceptionally fine walk at all times of the year. From the bustling harbour of Porthleven you take an easy coastal track with magnificent views across Mount's Bay. The sudden silence as one enters the wooded National Trust estate of Penrose contrasts sharply with the crashing of the mighty breakers driven onto Loe beach by the Atlantic swell. Penrose house is set in parkland backed by a colourful display of rhododendrons in the spring. There is even a hide in which to stand and watch the antics of the waterfowl on Loe Pool.

The Walk

From the pub turn left along the quay towards the clock tower. Turn left, following the coast road around the village. Continue along the coastal track until you reach a small car park.

Take the footpath from here, signposted 'Footpath to Loe Pool'. This soon joins another wide coastal track. Continue on this until you reach a large grey stone house on your left. You will now be overlooking Loe Pool and Bar.

This pool, actually the estuary of the river Cober, was created when a bar of sand was thrown up during a mighty storm in the Middle Ages. Helston was severely flooded and a way for the water to be released had to be made. In more recent times a culvert was constructed, enabling the river to flow underground, but one can well imagine the backbreaking work encountered by those digging a way through manually. The lovely, peaceful pool created by this phenomenon is not safe for swimming or fishing but provides an ideal habitat for various waterfowl and aquatic animals.

Turn away now from the magnificent coastline and walk inland through the gate beside the house. You are now in the Penrose Estate, owned by the National Trust. The wide gravel track is a pleasure to walk, with mixed woods on one side and the pool on the other. The track winds round, bringing fresh glimpses of the changing scenery. Penrose house and buildings

Penrose House and park. (The National Trust/Dan Flunder)

come into view and the track sweeps round to the right. At the T-junction turn left, signed 'Porthleven'.

You will cross a small granite bridge and will notice, just beyond it, a Victorian bath house. This has been restored by the National Trust and it is necessary to gain permission to view inside. It makes one appreciate the comfort in our present day bathrooms compared to the effort involved just over 100 years ago.

As the track forks, turn right. At the next fork turn left, and then right to a junction of roads. Take the one signed 'Loe Bar'. It is marginally nearer to walk directly back to Porthleven following the other road, however, there is no footpath and this road becomes very busy during the summer months.

Walk along the quiet 'Loe Bar' road, but at a left turn ignore the 'Bar' sign and walk straight on. You are now on the outskirts of the village. Follow the road, downhill into Porthleven, turning right to bring you back to the clock tower and the pub.

Places of interest nearby

Helston, 3 miles away, has a museum containing much to interest the historically minded. *Flambards Village* is just south of Helston.

Paul
14 The King's Arms

Just a mile from the well-known fishing village of Mousehole, the King's Arms is situated in the centre of Paul. An inn since 1756, it may have been the 'local' for Dolly Pentreath who was buried in the churchyard, opposite, in 1777. Her epitaph reads:

'Here lieth interred Dorothy Pentreath, said to have been the last person who conversed in the Ancient Cornish the peculiar language of this county from the earliest records till it expired in the late 18th century. This stone was erected by the Prince Louis Lucien Bonaparte in union with the vicar of St Paul, June 1860.'

The Cornish language has made some sort of come-back during the last few years, with occasional broadcasts and church services being held to encourage students to take part in the spoken as well as the written language.

This inn has progressed through the years from the days of

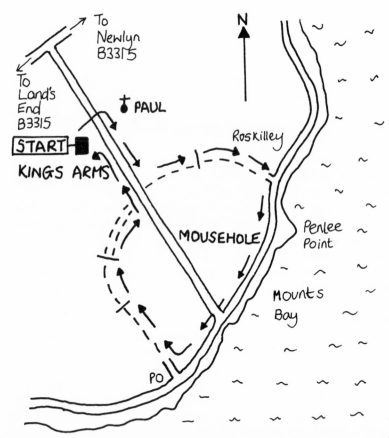

horse-drawn coaches to cater for the present day holiday trade. Still retaining its character, it is comfortably furnished, has a friendly atmosphere and offers a good choice of food and drink. As you would expect, seafood figures prominently on the menu but steaks and curries are also popular. Sandwiches, soup of the day, salads and ploughman's lunches, as well as vegetarian dishes, offer variety as bar meals. A children's menu caters for the youngsters' favourites. There is not a family room but there is space for children and they are made welcome. The well-kept real ales include Hicks, Bosun's and St Austell Mild, and the comprehensively-stocked bar caters for all tastes.

The pub is open on Monday to Saturday from 11 am to 3 pm and 6.30 pm to 11 pm, with the usual Sunday hours.

Telephone: 01736 731224.

How to get there: From Penzance take the coast road to Newlyn. Do not turn left into Newlyn village but continue straight on up a steep hill, the B3315. As the road levels out look for a turning on your left, signed 'Paul'. The pub is through the village, opposite the church.

Parking: There is plenty of parking space at the pub.

Length of the walk: 3 miles. Map: OS Landranger 203 Land's End and The Lizard (GR 465272).

Fields and pathways lead down to the sea at Roskilly. Pass the Penlee lifeboat station and go on into the delightful village of Mousehole. There is one short, steep climb as you leave Mousehole. Enjoy the views across to St Michael's Mount and the Lizard peninsula.
This is a walk of contrasts and one that most family groups should find pleasantly interesting.

The Walk
From the pub car park walk down the steps opposite the church. Turn right, down the hill, for about 150 yards until you see a footpath sign on your left. Cross the stile here and walk through the field, keeping the hedge on your right. At a gap, nearly at the bottom of the field, go into the adjacent field. The footpath goes diagonally across this field, but should it be cropped, walk round the lower end, following the left-hand hedge. Do not go through a gap in this hedge but continue round until you reach a granite step-stile. There are some buildings in front of you now. After crossing the stile, turn left, over a stream, and pass a house on your right. Continue gently uphill towards a farm. Turn left, passing between the house and buildings. Go through a wooden gate on your right. The path now passes beside converted barns. Keeping the hedge on your right, walk downhill towards the sea. Climb over a gate and, still keeping the hedge on your right, go over a stile into an enclosed path. Badger territory here . . .
Walk downhill to join the road, which is busy in summer. Cross over and turn right. This area is known as Roskilly.
You will very soon come to the Penlee lifeboat house and memorial to the men who were lost in the disaster of 1981.

St Michael's Mount from the sea. (The National Trust/Bill Newby)

Continue on the pavement until just before a 'road narrows' sign. Go down some steps on to the concrete path at beach level. Obviously, if there is a high tide or rough sea walk along the pavement into Mousehole village.

Proceed through the village along the coast road. I would not presume to advise you where to go in this delightful collection of narrow streets, craft shops and artists' galleries, quaint colourwashed cottages and enticing alleyways.

Make for the post office, situated almost at the end of the village. Immediately adjacent to the post office is a narrow lane, leading uphill, which ends in a row of cottages. Go up this and walk in front of the cottages. Continue on the path. At a junction turn right and take the path with the iron railings. There are harbour views from here. Go over the stile, not up the steps, and cross the field to a gap ahead. Now cross the next field, diagonally, to an iron gate. In the next field bear right to a gap and make for some houses and a stile in the right-hand corner. Climb the stile, pass through a gate and join an enclosed path. Paul church tower is now visible. Winter heliotrope borders this path, sweet smelling in the early part of the year.

On reaching the lane, turn left back to Paul and the car. An old wayside cross stands in the hedge on your right as you approach the village.

Places of interest nearby

Your glimpses of *St Michael's Mount* will probably encourage you to pay a visit to this 'jewel in the National Trust's crown'. Stop awhile in Newlyn to see the fishing fleet anchored in the harbour alongside the famous fish market. This far west part of Cornwall has *Land's End* as its mecca, which has much to offer young and old alike. Penzance with its old buildings and busy harbour is never short of interest. St Michael's Mount should not be missed. Try to go at low tide and walk across the causeway, many of the stones were placed there by monks from the Benedictine Priory, founded by Edward the Confessor.

⑮ Zennor
The Tinners Arms

Built of local granite, this 13th century building merges well
with its moorland setting. Constructed as a hostelry to house
the men engaged on building the nearby church, it has been an
inn since that time. Change comes slowly to this far western
part of Cornwall. The name is a reminder of the tin mining
industry which flourished until the mid 19th century. Even
today, the odd chimney stack still stands, isolated and strangely
beautiful with its clinging ivy and brambles. The medieval field
patterns of the farms are all around as you drive along the coast
road from St Ives to St Just. It says much for this pub that in no
way has it attempted to change its image but instead blends
easily with the landscape. A visit to the church reminds us of the
Mermaid of Zennor legend. There is a carved bench end to
which hangs a tale. It represents the traditional mermaid who is
said to have once visited this church, attracted by the
marvellous singing of the squire's son. She was so captivated

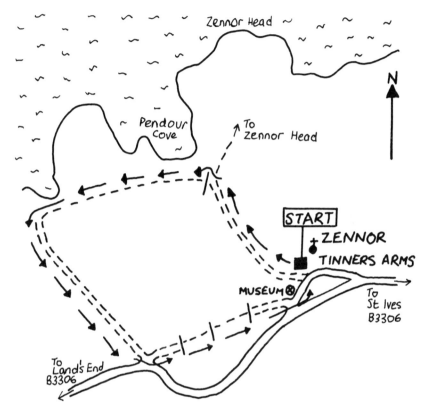

that she enticed him to return with her to the sea. It is said that if you listen carefully above Pendour Cove you will still hear singing . . .

A friendly welcome awaits you at the Tinners Arms. The stone floor and granite fireplace, the low beams and well-worn settles help to make it a comfortable, hospitable place. Ploughman's lunches, smoked mackerel, crab sandwiches and salads and a daily 'Blackboard Special' menu offer snacks and meals to please everyone. Treacle nut tart or hot apple pie with cream should tempt the pudding eaters amongst you. Children can be accommodated in the room away from the bar. A large flower-bordered patio offers a pleasant place where they can play and adults can enjoy a drink and meal during the summer months. This freehouse serves Cornish ale brewed in oak casks.

71

The Wayside Museum and water wheel at Zennor.

Hicks Special Draught, St Austell ale, Flowers Original and Poachers are other brews. There is a selection of lagers and ciders and a good house wine.

The pub is open from 11 am to 3 pm and 7 pm to 11 pm, with the usual Sunday hours.

Telephone: 01736 796927.

How to get there: Zennor lies on the B3306 St Ives to St Just road. The pub is opposite the church.

Parking: There is parking at the pub. A nearby free car park is also available.

Length of the walk: 2½ miles. Map: OS Landranger 203 Land's End and The Lizard (GR 453385).

The breathtaking coastal scenery more than compensates for the rather rough steps encountered as you begin the short distance of coastal path. Look down on Pendour Cove of Mermaid fame and enjoy the field paths and tracks on the return route. Stop at the Wayside Museum to see the oldest private collection of artefacts, which covers every aspect of life in Zennor and district from 3000 BC to the 1930s.

While most family groups should be able to cope with the short steep slope of the coastal path it is not suitable for the very young. Wear good walking shoes or boots. An alternative would be to walk out onto Zennor Head where seats are provided by the National Trust and the views are magnificent.

The Walk

From the pub turn left and walk between the church and the pub. Turn left again, almost immediately, passing a coastguard look-out house on your left. The lane leads to the coastal path, indicated by a waymark stone.

This is the point from which you can go out onto Zennor Head. If you wish to do this, walk straight ahead, following the marked path.

For the circular walk, turn left here and descend some steep steps to Pendour Cove. Cross a small stream. Follow the path across the slope, turn left and walk uphill to a seat. The path skirts steep slopes. Follow it down to the next headland, with superb views. Continue round the base of the headland. Where the path divides, by some rocky pillars, take the left-hand branch that leads uphill. Continue round the back wall of a cottage. Join the track that leads inland past old tin mine workings. There are views across to Gurnards Head from here.

Proceed along the track until almost reaching the coast road. Turn left, passing immediately in front of some cottages. Where the track swings sharply to the left, go straight ahead over a granite stile. Cross a second stile and go past an open gateway, with the hedge on your left. Cross another stile and continue straight ahead to the next stile. Keep Zennor church tower directly in front of you. Go across the next field and over a stile, then cross two fields, walking slightly diagonally right, to a final stile.

Make for some farm buildings ahead and join a farm lane. It can be muddy here during wet weather. At the road turn left. The museum will be on your left as you walk down the hill back to the pub.

16 Lelant
The Badger Inn

A long history is attached to this comfortable pub and hotel. An inn in 1700, it became known as the Prades Arms when owned by a London company of that name. Lelant Hotel followed, but for the last eight years it has been the Badger Inn. Lelant parish is one of many in the county which suffered from accumulations of sand. In these more enlightened days, marram grass is planted to stabilise the dunes. It is, however, quite obvious how the estuary of the river Hayle has silted up over the years despite various attempts to dredge and make safe the shifting sands. The ancient pilgrim's trail to St Michael's Mount passes through Lelant, close to the church. It is interesting to read the notice and map on display outside. A blacksmith's shop was once located next door to the inn, no doubt a useful addition to the services offered to the traveller at the hostelry.

A wide choice of dishes is available at the Badger, including fish, chicken and grills. There are four fillings to choose from in a three-egg omelette, also salads, sandwiches, hot bar snacks

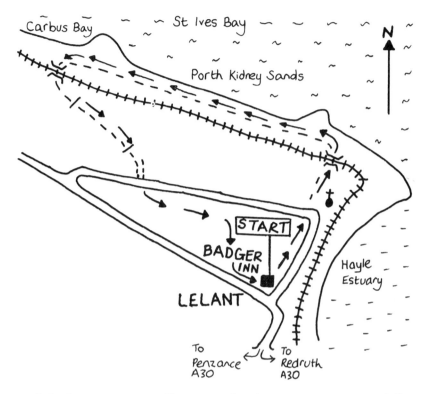

and jacket potatoes. Home-made desserts are a speciality, served with a generous portion of clotted cream. Children are welcome and have their own menu, containing all the favourite meals. It is not very often that one sees a 'baby bowl of fresh vegetables and gravy' on offer. A good pint is served from a choice of Wreckers, Tinners and Duchy real ales. Scrumpy Jack cider, Guinness and Murphy's are on draught. Wine is served by the glass and bottle at competitive prices. A spacious lounge overlooks the garden, and accommodation is also available in well-furnished, en suite rooms.

The opening times are 11.30 am to 3 pm and 6 pm to 11.30 pm, with the usual Sunday hours.

Telephone: 01736 752181.

How to get there: Lelant lies on the A3074, off the A30 at the western end of the Hayle bypass. The road is signed 'St Ives'.

75

Parking: A large car park is available at the pub.

Length of the walk: 2¾ miles or 3¾ miles if you include a detour to Carbis Bay. Map: OS Landranger 203 Land's End and The Lizard (GR 545371).

A lovely walk along the Hayle estuary at first, with views to Godrevy lighthouse and St Ives. Trencrom Hill towers above the village, with its neolithic camp on the summit. Footpaths and bridleways are well marked and easy to follow and the route is suitable for all ages and family groups.

A detour can be made down into Carbis Bay where refreshments are available during the summer months. A wide sandy beach makes it a good place to pause awhile, perhaps even for a paddle or swim . . .

The Walk

From the pub car park walk down the road signed to the golf course and church. On reaching the church you will see a coastal footpath sign passing to the left of the churchyard. As the path ends and a track leads to left and right walk straight ahead towards a concrete tower. You are now on the edge of the golf course – take care, flying golf balls could be about. Go under the railway bridge. This is the line used as the park and ride route from St Erth to St Ives. Turn left, following the coastal path sign. You are now overlooking the Hayle estuary and Godrevy lighthouse. St Ives lies ahead.

Keep to the path through the dunes. At a fork take the top path, with Porth Kidney sands below. You are now on a really pretty coastal path, with buddleia, ferns and overhanging bushes and trees. This area is known as 'The Nutgrove'. St Uny's Well is located here, although it is difficult to find during the lush summer months.

At the top of this path cross the railway line, carefully. This is where you can make the detour to Carbis Bay. Afterwards you will need to retrace your steps to this point.

After crossing the railway line, to continue the main walk, turn right past some houses. At the top of the drive turn left at a footpath sign. Go through the car park of the Sea Urchin apartments to another footpath sign. Pass over a wooden bridge to a seat where you may like to take in the views along the coast. The path narrows and passes between two hedges. Follow the

Inland scenery near the Carn Brea mining area.

path as it bears right, through a kissing-gate. The golf course is below. Emerge from the path onto the golf course – careful! Keep to the right, following the grey concrete blocks. Pass a seat and make for the top right-hand corner. Go through the gate and onto a track. Turn left.

At the lane, turn left again. Notice the old Cornish wayside cross originally set up in AD 900 to guide travellers using the pilgrims' trail to St Michael's Mount. Walk down the road as far as the golf club buildings. There is a footpath sign opposite.

Follow this sign, through the gate and across a field, keeping to the left-hand hedge. Go over a granite step stile into the adjacent field. Keep straight on to the next granite stile. Go over that and on to the next, visible, stile. Cross this, close to some buildings and continue to a layby. Turn left onto the A3074 for about 200 yards and so back to the pub.

Places of interest nearby

St Ives, which beckons ahead on the outward route of your walk. It is only a short drive from Lelant.

St Agnes
The Peterville Inn

The Peterville Inn is in a hamlet of the same name, between St Agnes and Trevaunance Cove. St Agnes Beacon dominates this area – a high granitic outcrop, hence the mineralisation of the region. Now a holiday beach, Trevaunance Cove was once the centre of a much mined area. The inn has a welcoming appearance, with baskets and tubs of flowers outside, and low beams and a granite fireplace inside. A roaring log fire will greet customers during the winter, while a roof garden will attract them during the summer. It is rumoured that a ghost, believed to be the spirit of Dick Argall, a landlord some 200 years ago, causes a few 'happenings' to occur . . .

The Peterville is a popular, busy pub where good food is served both at lunchtime and in the evening. The carvery area has seating for 32, while bar fare can be eaten in the lounges.

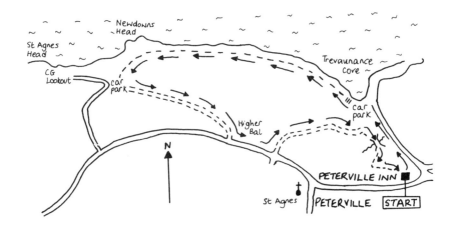

The soup of the day comes highly recommended and among the snacks are sandwiches, pasties, sausage, egg and chips and a variety of salads. For the ale drinkers there is Newquay Steam, together with Cornish Bitter, Marston's Pedigree and Boddingtons. The lagers available are Heineken, Stella Artois and Steam Pils. Children are welcome and should enjoy the roof top garden during the summer months.

The pub is open from 12 noon to 3 pm every day. In the evenings the opening times are 5 pm to 11 pm on weekdays and 7 pm to 10 pm on Sundays.

Telephone: 01872 552406.

How to get there: St Agnes lies west of the A30 Bodmin to Redruth road. Take the B3277 from the roundabout at Three Burrows. Continue along this road until reaching the village of St Agnes. Turn right at the church, downhill for about ¼ mile. The Peterville Inn is on your left at the bottom of the hill.

Parking: At the pub. There is also parking at Trevaunance Cove.

Length of the walk: 4 miles. Map: OS Landranger 204 Truro, Falmouth and surrounding area and OS Landranger 203 Land's End and The Lizard (GR 725507).

Portreath harbour.

This walk offers you scenic views across windblown headlands. Watch the swimmers and surfers enjoying the pleasures of Trevaunance Cove. There is clifftop walking for some of the way. Explore the paths and tracks of the village, with the Beacon towering above.

This 4 mile circular route with its short, steep climb up some steps, will be enjoyed by families with older children (perhaps over ten years of age).

The Walk

From the pub car park turn left, then immediately left again into Quay Road. Walk down the road, watching out for the traffic during the summer months, until you reach the Driftwood Spars pub on your right. Turn left here for a few yards until you see a coastal path sign on your right. Take this track and continue to follow the coastal path signs, passing a hotel on your right with magnificent views across Trevaunance Cove and the coastline.

Climb some rather steep steps for about 50 yards and keep to the right, passing a capped mine shaft on your left. At a bench, thoughtfully provided at just the right spot, join a track and keep along the coast. On reaching a fork keep to the right, by an acorn sign and bench. At the next fork keep on the lower path and bear to the right at the next fork, with a bench ahead, on to Newdowns Head. Keep straight on where the path divides, making towards the coastguard station. At the next fork, just before an acorn post, turn left.

The coastal path goes on over St Agnes Head, but we leave it here. As the path forks again, turn left onto a gravelled parking area. The car track goes to the right but you turn left onto an unmade track. You can see it wending its way towards St Agnes Beacon, which now towers ahead. In about ¼ mile you will reach a road.

Turn left and continue along the lane until you reach a group of houses known as Higher Bal. Turn left here and in a few yards turn right along a stony track until reaching a road. Turn right.

Walk along the pavement here until you reach a left turn, Rocky Lane, and a sign to 'Wheal Friendly Chalet Park'. The road bends to the right and downhill. Pass the chalet park on your right and look for a parking restriction sign also on your right. Turn right here into a coppice and follow the footpath, passing several benches until you reach a flight of steps. Go down these onto a lane. Turn right. You are now back on the lane you came down at the beginning of the walk.

In about 200 yards, on reaching a bench, turn right over a stream. As the path forks, by another bench, turn left, passing two houses. As you reach the bottom of the track past the houses turn right over a bridge and stream. This pretty pathway alongside the stream continues for about 200 yards until you reach a clearance. Make for the right-hand corner and a granite stile. Once over this, you will find yourselves in the pub yard.

Places of interest nearby

St Agnes Leisure Park offers many delights for children. You may care to walk up St Agnes Beacon where a panorama will stretch before you including, on a clear day, 17 churches. Drive west along the coast road to Portreath where a traditional Cornish harbour was constructed during the days of sailing ships as a safe anchorage for those bringing in coal from Wales and for sending out the copper and tin. The Pepper Pot, a day-mark at the entrance, guided ships round the rocky coastline into the harbour.

18 West Pentire
The Bowgie

West Pentire is a hamlet lying to the west of the major holiday resort of Newquay. A few houses, bungalows, a shop/café, a hotel and the pub all overlook the superb surfing beach of Crantock Bay. A former cowshed, hence the Cornish name of 'Bowgie', this attractive inn became a small village club some 40 years ago. From these beginnings it has evolved into the present comfortable, welcoming hostelry it is today.

Several bars with open fireplaces and walls decorated with local pictorial history are complemented by a 'Surfers' bar and a well organised family room. Contrary to many such rooms, the accent has been placed on accommodating the younger members of the family in comfort and spaciousness, with a sea view from most of the windows. On summer days the children can enjoy playing out of doors on swings, models and wooden climbing frames. Warm, comfortable bars and lounges all offer a scenic place to enjoy the food and drink offered at this pub, which must surely lay claim to having some of the best coastal scenery in Cornwall. Available during all opening times, the menu is varied and generously served. Ratatouille with crusty bread is a firm favourite, as is fishermen's platter and turkey and ham pie. Sandwiches and salads, a variety of vegetarian dishes and a 'Blackboard Special' which changes daily complete the menu... except for the sweets. Toffee, apple and pecan pie or treacle tart with cream are but two of the choices... slimmers beware! A children's menu offers the youngsters their favourite foods at a modest price. The Bowgie is a freehouse and serves well-kept real ales. Flowers and Boddingtons are always available, supplemented by a guest beer. Bowgie Bitter is the local brew. Draught Guinness, Scrumpy Jack cider, Castlemaine and Carlsberg lagers are also served.

The opening times are 11 am to 3 pm and 6 pm to 11 pm in the winter on weekdays and 11 am to 11 pm in the summer. The Sunday hours are 12.30 pm to 3 pm and 7 pm to 10.30 pm throughout the year. Food is served during the week from 11 am to 2.30 pm and 6 pm to 10 pm, throughout the year. Telephone: 01637 830363.

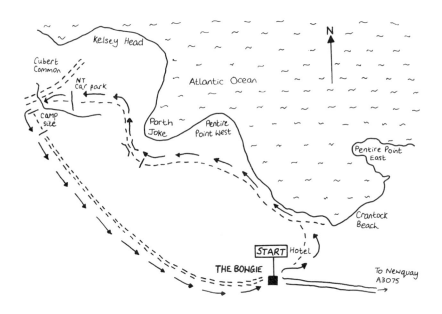

How to get there: The Bowgie lies on the seaward side of the A3075 Newquay to Redruth road. From Newquay take the first turn to the right after the Trevemper roundabout, signed 'Crantock'. Follow the signs for Crantock but do not turn down into the village. Keep straight on until the road ends. The pub will be immediately ahead of you.

Parking: There is ample parking at the pub.

Length of the walk: 3 miles. Map: OS Landranger 200 Newquay and Bodmin (GR 775608).

Inland paths and soft-turfed headlands, a sheltered cove and short stretch of hedged coastal path make this a walk suitable for all ages and abilities. Sea and sand, flowers and surfers, this route has them all, along with pleasant places to relax on both clifftop and beach.

The Walk

Leave the car park by the main entrance, pass the Crantock Bay Hotel on your left and take the footpath signed 'To the Beach'. From here you will be able to appreciate the full beauty of Crantock Beach, famous for surfing. One may well be forgiven for thinking that it is seals that are transporting themselves among the waves rather than the wet suited surfers who are pitting their strength and ability against the mighty Atlantic rollers. Spring and summer, autumn and winter, very few are the days that find this beach devoid of these dedicated sportsmen.

A swift oncoming tide and the river Gannel to the east of the beach necessitates the presence of patrolling lifeguards during the holiday months of May to September.

When the footpath forks, take the left-hand path away from the beach. Now follow the coastal path for a short distance through the garden of the hotel. Go over a stile and bear right. You are now at the bottom of the Bowgie car park.

Continue bearing to the right until you are on the headland of West Pentire. Do not follow the coastal path around the seaward side but, instead, cross the headland at the widest central part. This makes for easy walking on the soft turf and provides an area where the children can run around.

Surfers on Crantock beach. (Restormel Borough Council)

It is here that, during the spring and summer, you should find an abundance of the wild flowers particularly suited to the conditions of wind and salt laden air. There are the tiny blue flowers of squill, so beautiful as they cling to the close-packed moss, sea pink or thrift and tiny yellow trefoil plants that give colour to the grassy slopes.

After crossing the open top of the headland, pass into the adjacent field and walk downhill, keeping to the right. You are now overlooking Porth Joke. Porth is the Cornish word for beach or cove and while the meaning of Joke is obscure, it is thought to come from the Cornish word Jouk – to duck, making Porth Joke a bathing beach or cove. Follow the path round the field and through the gate. Turn right, continuing alongside the hedge until reaching a wooden gate leading onto the beach. Go through this and over a wooden bridge. The beach now stretches away to the right, shadowed by the area known as 'The Kelseys' and Cubert Common.

Both headland and common are ancient burial sites with their rounded tumuli and long barrows. It is believed that the nearer the sea a tumulus is, the more important the person was. Legend has it that should one of the tumuli on Cubert

85

Common be disturbed then disaster will befall Cubert village. True or not, these graves have been undisturbed for several thousand years...

After crossing the bridge turn left, following the sandy path through a gate. This path now wends its way inland alongside a stream. The next gate leads into a small National Trust car park, the nearest vehicular access to the beach. Go through the car park onto a farm track. Turn left. Take the path, on your left, immediately adjacent to a farm gate marked 'Camping Site'. This path passes between the farmhouse and the camp site.

You will now reach a concrete driveway. Bear to the left and walk uphill for a short distance. At the top go between two sets of farm buildings and onto a tarmac road. Keep to the right, the shop/café is on your right and the entrance to the Bowgie car park on your left.

⑲ St Mawgan
The Falcon

Set in the beautiful Vale of Lanherne, it is not surprising that the Falcon attracts people from a wide area of Cornwall. Although close to the St Mawgan airfield and passsenger flight terminal it is amazing how little impact this facility has had on the rural atmosphere of the area. St Mawgan is a village in the true sense, with two shops, a post office, a village school, a playing field and both Catholic and Anglican churches. A craft shop is tucked away near the river while a bonsai nursery is close by. A ford and footbridge trace the route of the old road. The history of the pub takes us back to the 16th century. Formerly called the Gardeners Arms, it is known to have been a hostelry since 1758. A falcon features in its crest. This bird was a symbol of a meeting place for Roman Catholics during the Reformation. A falcon would be flown, giving the signal that it was safe to meet for a secret service.

The Falcon is well known for its food and a blackboard menu

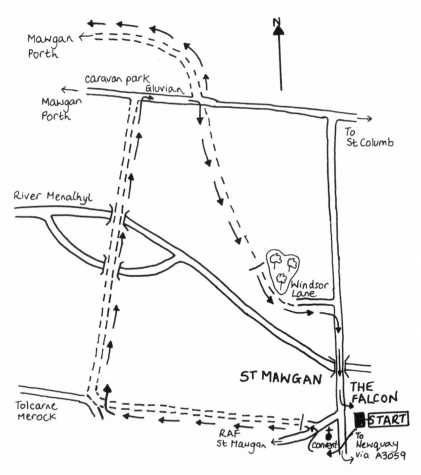

offers such dishes as fresh local fish, lamb and cranberry casserole or ham and mushroom au gratin. Two or three vegetarian dishes are prepared each day. Locally made pasties, sandwiches and salads are served in the bar. Children are accommodated in the large dining area where they have a menu of their own. Barbecues are a feature on summer evenings, sometimes accompanied by music. There are also four letting bedrooms, two of which are en suite. A St Austell house, the real ales include XXXX Mild, Tinners Ale and Hicks Special Draught. A selection of lagers, Strongbow and Guinness on draught are also included in the well-stocked bar. The 10 malt whiskies and a 26-bin wine list are the pride of the landlord. Take a look at the paintings in the dining room, all done by one artist of mostly local scenes.

The pub is open on weekdays from 11 am to 3 pm and 6 pm to 11 pm, and on Sundays from 12 noon to 3 pm and 7 pm to 10.30 pm.

Telephone: 01637 860225.

How to get there: St Mawgan lies 6 miles north-east of Newquay. Take the A3059 from Newquay and continue, passing RAF St Mawgan on your left. Just past the runways, look for a turn on your left, signed 'St Mawgan'. A turn to the right in about 1 ½ miles takes you into the village centre.

Parking: There is a large car park at the inn and a parking area behind the post office.

Length of the walk: 2 miles, or 4 miles if you include a detour to Mawgan Porth. Map: OS Landranger 200 Newquay and Bodmin (GR 876659).

This is an easy circular route with the option of a detour into the coastal village of Mawgan Porth. The river Menalhyl affords a focal point as it meanders through this lovely valley. I saw a buzzard swoop for its prey – and squirrels race madly up a tree when they were disturbed. While you are always conscious that the sea is 'just over there', this country walk along an old parish road provides a sheltered route for those blustery days.

The Walk

On a bank above the church stands Lanherne. This house was formerly the seat of the Arundells, a great Cornish family. In 1794 it became the home of a community of Carmelite nuns. It is opposite this beautiful building that our walk begins.

Cross the road from the pub and walk through the gate to the left of a driveway to the convent. Bear left as you reach the house, following the stone wall round to the road. Turn right for a few yards and cross over. Next to a farm a wooden five-barred gate leads into a field along an old parish road. There are white road markings as it adjoins the lane. This is a gated road and care should be taken to leave the gates as you find them.

A nearby attraction is the river Gannel, south of Newquay.

This pleasant lane takes you slightly uphill, overlooking the valley, with glimpses of the sea in the distance.

As you approach a farmhouse on your left, Tolcarne Merock, turn right and walk downhill towards a ford. Cross this via the footbridge and walk on to another wooden bridge over the river. Continue uphill, passing some buildings on your right until you reach a road. Take care, this carries a considerable amount of holiday traffic in the summer. Turn right.

In about 200 yards look for a footpath sign on your right. This is where you can make your detour to Mawgan Porth. To do so, take the metalled track on your left and follow the signs for 'Gluvian' and 'Mawgan Porth'. This soon becomes a sandy track. Retrace your steps to this point after visiting the long sandy beach.

To continue the main walk, climb the stile opposite the turning to Mawgan Porth, into a field. There is a wide, mown path with the river on your right. Keep below a slight earth bank on your left. Make for a stile ahead. Having crossed the stile, the path narrows between low bushes. It could be muddy here during wet weather. Cross a granite stile, continue to a wooden gate and emerge onto a narrow, tarred road, Windsor Lane. Turn left. This lovely lane, bordered by trees and flowers, leads to a junction with the road down into St Mawgan village. Turn right and walk past the playing field, over the bridge to the church and pub.

It would be a pity to miss the opportunity to visit the church. There is old woodwork in the screen, pulpit and bench ends. The family tree of the Arundell family makes fascinating reading. The churchyard contains interesting memorials and an unusual lantern cross.

Places of interest nearby

St Mawgan itself has much to offer, while nearby Newquay with its world famous beaches is full of indoor and outdoor 'things to do'. The *Cornish Shire Horse Centre* is just over 4 miles away, at Tredinnick.

20 Padstow
The Old Custom House

Padstow is one of Cornwall's oldest towns. It was little known until the advent of the railway during the late 1800s. Situated on the Camel estuary, it has long been a seafaring place and is now a busy harbour, with fishing boats vying for moorings along the extended quay. Investment by the EC provided a much improved harbour and were it not for the sand bar which stretches across the estuary mouth much larger craft would be able to make use of this natural haven. Known locally as the 'Doom Bar', it has lived up to its name on many past occasions. Padstow celebrates May Day with a time honoured celebration known as Hobby Hoss Day. Two 'hosses' now parade the streets on that day with their unwieldy skirts and grotesque masks. The ceremony dates from 1346 when the creature (there was only one in those days) was supposed to have frightened away Frenchmen who appeared outside Padstow during the siege of Calais. Whatever its origin, it is cause for a good day's fun for both locals and visitors.

The Old Custom House pub comprises three buildings built in the 1800s. It was originally the customs and excise house and is now listed as a building of historical interest. It occupies a fine position in the centre of the town, overlooking the harbour. Spacious rooms and comfortable furnishings make this a pleasant place to eat and drink. There are also 27 tastefully furnished and equipped bedrooms, all of which are en suite. Most have harbour and estuary views. An elegant dining room offers an excellent à la carte and table d'hôte menu. There is an extensive choice of fresh fish and seafood dishes as the restaurant makes good use of local catches. The wine list maintains a selection to suit most tastes. The bar menu, both at lunchtime and in the evening, offers a variety of generously-portioned meals. Local food is used whenever possible and again fresh fish is featured. A 'Blackboard Special' menu changes daily but ploughman's and fisherman's lunches are always available, as are various vegetarian dishes. Children are catered for with their own menu. Most 'favourites' are available and can be eaten in the large family room adjacent to the bar. Families are also welcome to use the comfortable conservatory. The beers served are Tinners and Bosun's, both real ales, while keg Wreckers and Duchy are other choices. There are several lagers, along with the usual spirits.

The opening times are 11 am to 11 pm on weekdays, with the usual Sunday opening hours. Lunches are served from 12 noon to 2 pm, cream teas from 3 pm to 5 pm and evening meals from 7 pm to 9 pm.
Telephone: 01841 532359.

How to get there: From Wadebridge, take the A39, travelling south-west. In about 3 miles, after passing the Agricultural Show Ground, look for the junction with the A389, signed 'Padstow'. Take this road and continue on it until reaching the town. Follow the 'town centre' signs (one-way system) until reaching the harbour car park. Leave your car there and walk across the road to the Old Custom House.

Parking: There is no car park at the pub. Car parks are numerous but the one suggested above is nearest.

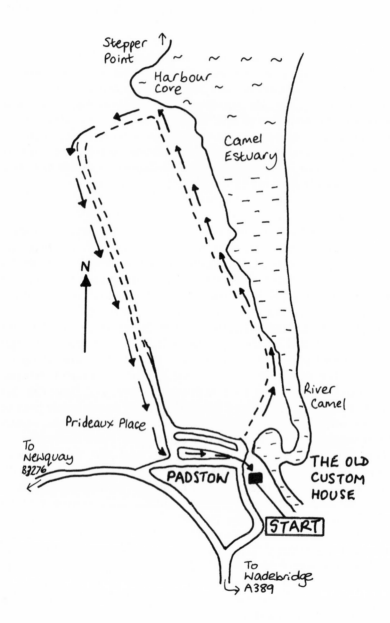

Stepper
Point

Harbour
Cove

Camel
Estuary

N

Prideaux Place

To
Newquay
B3276

PADSTOW

River
Camel

THE OLD
CUSTOM
HOUSE

START

To
Wadebridge
A389

Length of the walk: 2½ miles. Map: OS Landranger 200 Newquay and Bodmin (GR 918755).

The estuary of the river Camel has a particular charm of its own. This walk explores the paths along the shore and returns by a farm road. Sandy beaches, dunes and fields all entice one away from the easily-defined footpath.

Not only do we have the opportunity to enjoy some most spectacular scenery but also the chance to visit the lovely old house of Prideaux Place. Check times of opening at the information centre before leaving Padstow. Among the sights and sounds of the working harbour are the crab and lobster holding tanks, filled with their long-clawed inhabitants. You will find these adjacent to the old train station buildings.

The Walk

Leave Padstow by walking along the harbour towards the quay. Either cross the harbour entrance on the new lock bridge or walk round by the road. Considerable investment has created a harbour which can retain its water at all states of the tide. As you approach the slipway adjacent to the information centre, leave the road and take the left fork, signed 'coastpath'.

Keep to this tarmacked path as it wends gently uphill. Pass the war memorial and go through the gate. This is a good vantage point from which to enjoy views across to the sailing village of Rock and the sands of Daymer Bay. St Enodoc church steeple peeps out of the sand dunes almost opposite. It is here that Sir John Betjeman is buried and where he spent many hours pacing the coastline as he put thoughts into words to create the verses which were to make him such a celebrated Poet Laureate.

The fluttering sails of the dinghies and the more stately passage of the working boats will entertain you as you walk along the now widening path of the estuary. In summer, a beach below or the warm sand of the dunes may tempt you to sunbathe for a while at this point.

The path now skirts Harbour Cove. The lifeboat house ahead is disused these days. The silting of the estuary along with the necessity for larger lifeboats made it impracticable to continue the service in this location. The lifeboat is now housed at Trevose Head, where the lighthouse and coastguard station were already established.

Stepper Point, with its day-mark tower looms ahead – a

Padstow harbour.

rather formidable climb and one we shall not be pursuing today...

You will now see a wide track, making inland, away from the coastal path. Take this, leading to Tregirls Farm. The route is slightly uphill, but easily walked. On reaching the farm, bear left into a lane. This a farm road and, as such, carries very little traffic. Ignore all footpath signs and keep to the lane. In about ½ mile you will reach Prideaux Place on your right. You may be fortunate enough to catch a glimpse of a herd of deer in the field opposite.

Take either of the next two turnings on your left. The second one takes you past the church but both lead back into town by way of the delightful narrow streets winding down to the harbour.